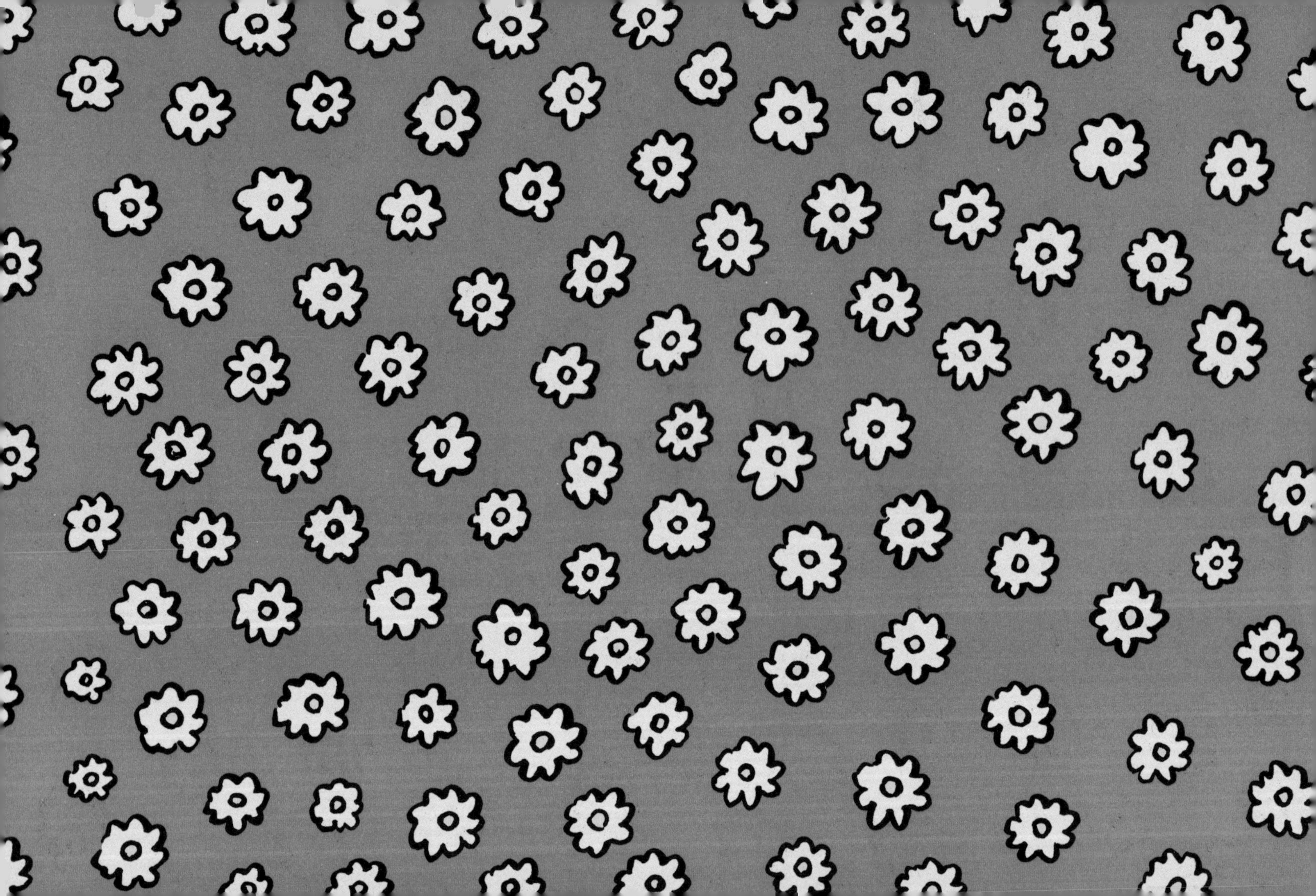

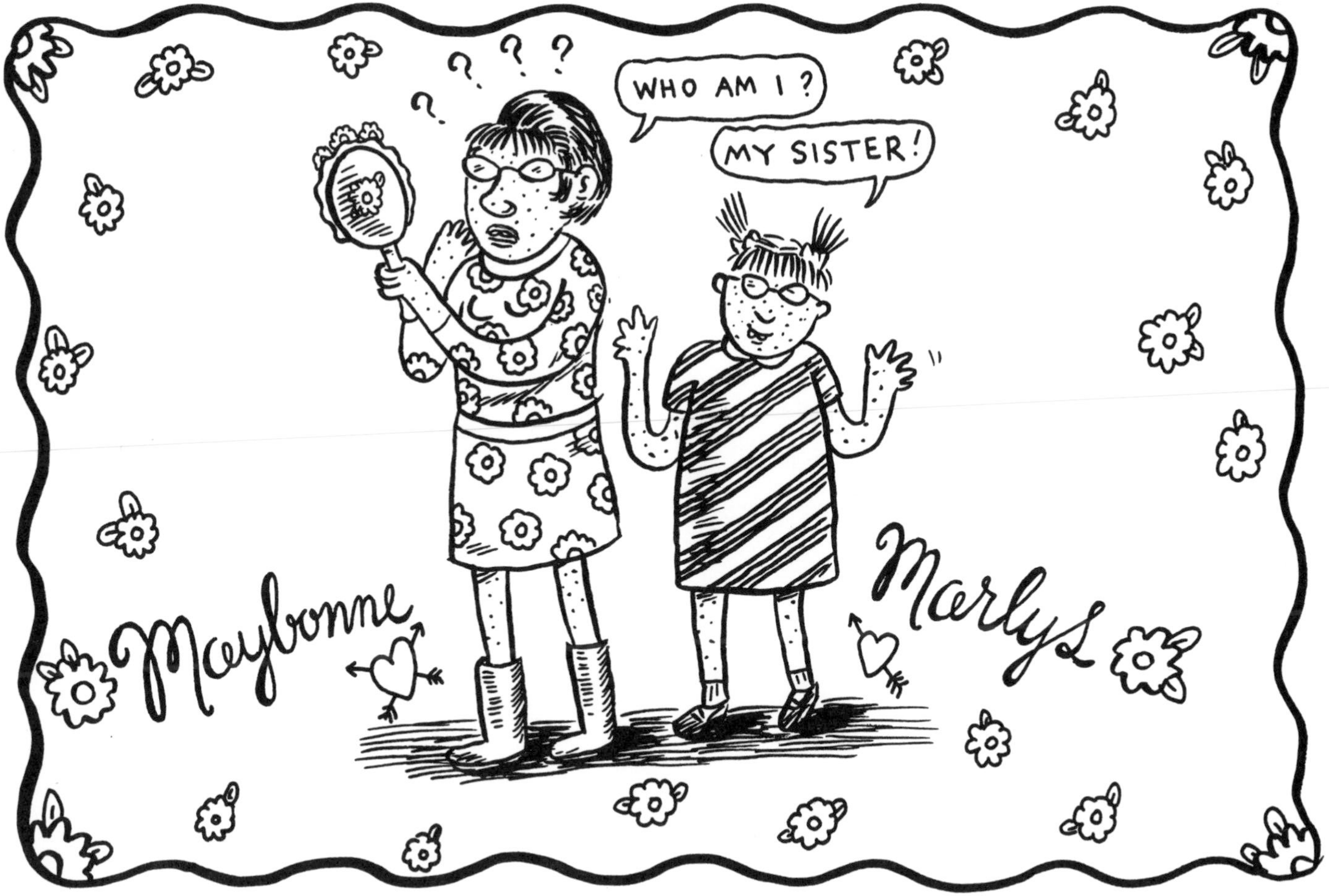
WHO AM I?
MY SISTER!
Maybonne
Marlys

COME OVER COME OVER

LYNDA ❀ BARRY

Drawn & Quarterly

This book is dedicated to Robert Roth ♡ and ♡ the city of Chicago

drawnandquarterly.com

ISBN 978-1-77046-545-9 • First edition: January 2022
Printed in China • 10 9 8 7 6 5 4 3 2 1

Cataloguing data available from Library and Archives Canada

Published in the USA by Drawn & Quarterly, a client publisher of
Farrar, Straus and Giroux. Published in Canada by Drawn & Quarterly, a
client publisher of Raincoast Books. Published in the United Kingdom
by Drawn & Quarterly, a client publisher of Publishers Group UK.

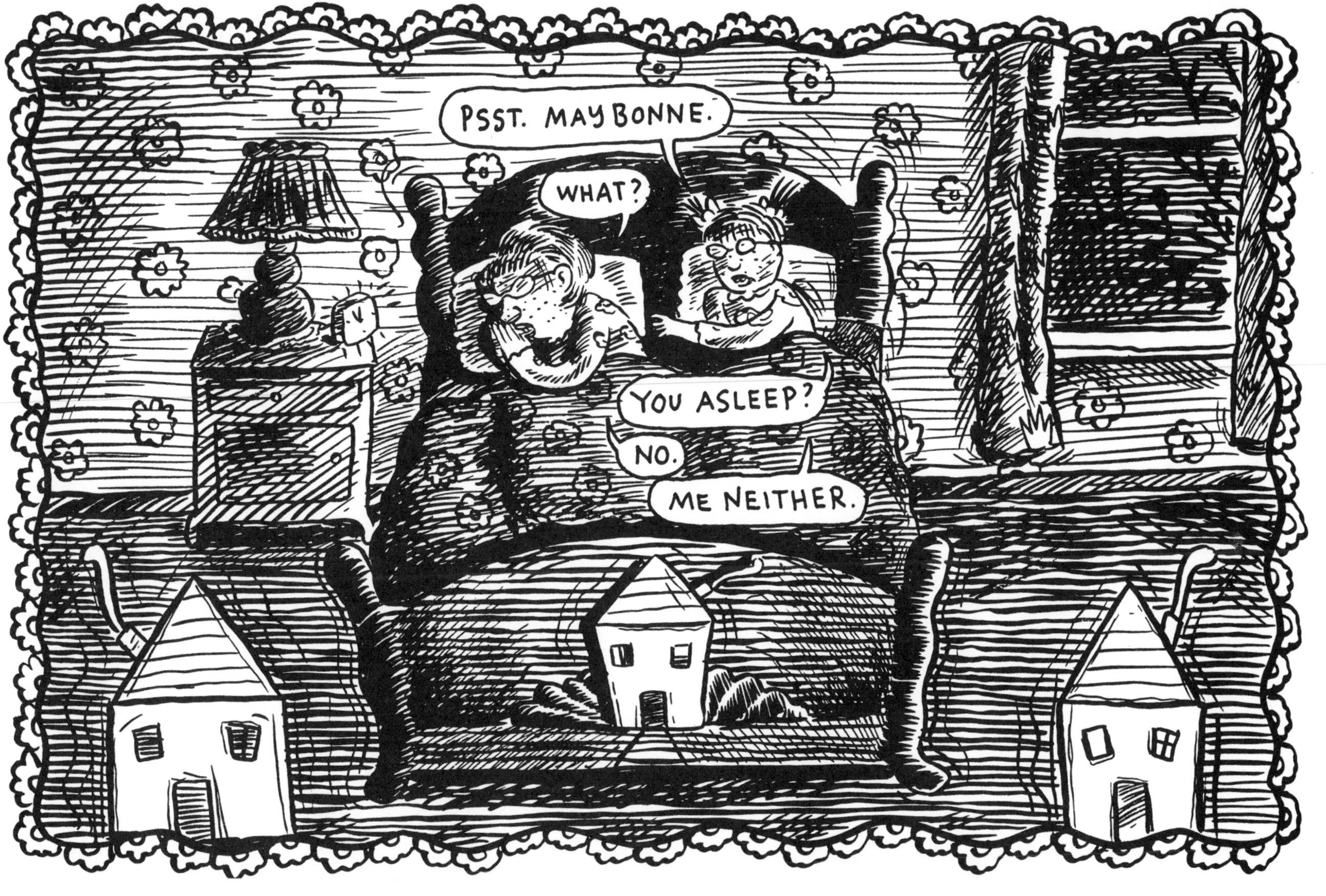
PSST. MAYBONNE.
WHAT?
YOU ASLEEP?
NO.
ME NEITHER.

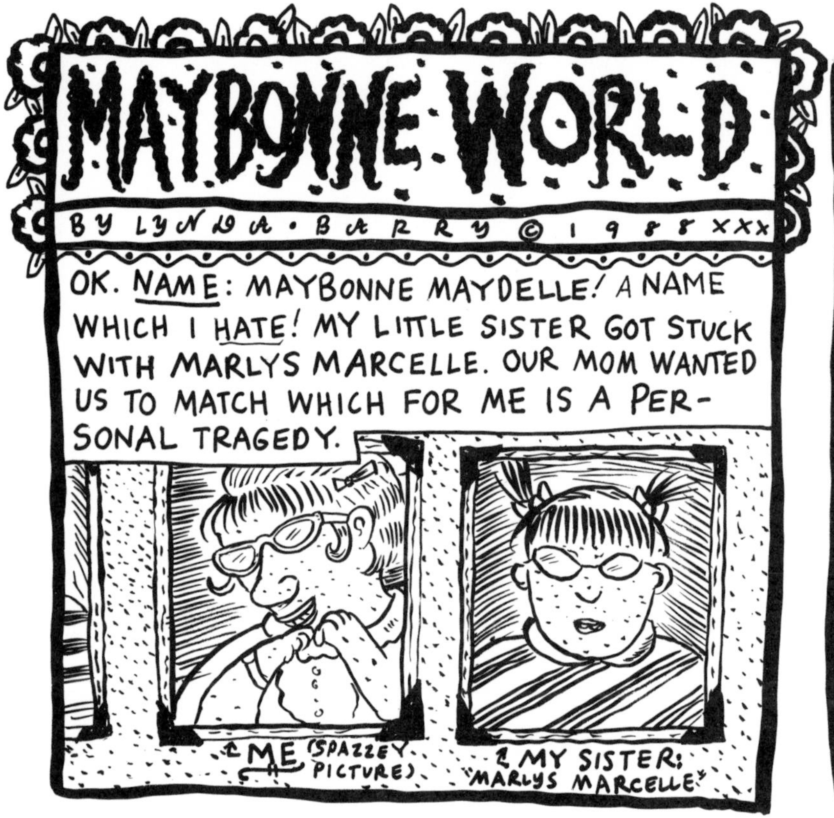
MAYBONNE WORLD
BY LYNDA BARRY © 1988 XXX
OK. NAME: MAYBONNE MAYDELLE! A NAME WHICH I HATE! MY LITTLE SISTER GOT STUCK WITH MARLYS MARCELLE. OUR MOM WANTED US TO MATCH WHICH FOR ME IS A PERSONAL TRAGEDY.
ME (SPAZZEY PICTURE)
MY SISTER: "MARLYS MARCELLE"

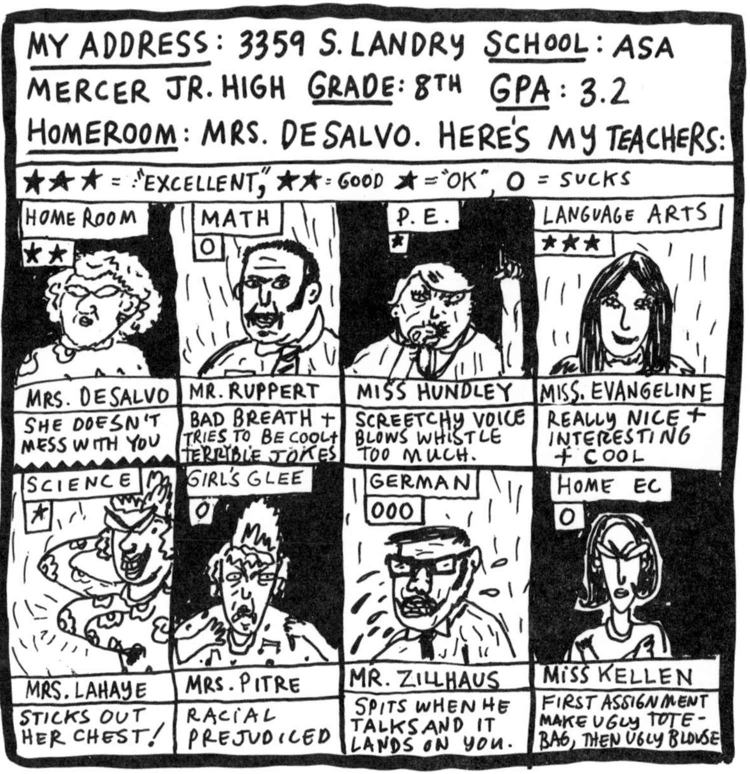
MY ADDRESS: 3359 S. LANDRY SCHOOL: ASA MERCER JR. HIGH GRADE: 8TH GPA: 3.2 HOMEROOM: MRS. DESALVO. HERE'S MY TEACHERS:
★★★ = "EXCELLENT," ★★ = GOOD ★ = "OK", O = SUCKS
HOME ROOM
★★
MRS. DESALVO
SHE DOESN'T MESS WITH YOU
MATH
O
MR. RUPPERT
BAD BREATH + TRIES TO BE COOL + TERRIBLE JOKES
P.E.
★
MISS HUNDLEY
SCREETCHY VOICE BLOWS WHISTLE TOO MUCH.
LANGUAGE ARTS
★★★
MISS. EVANGELINE
REALLY NICE + INTERESTING + COOL
SCIENCE
★
MRS. LAHAYE
STICKS OUT HER CHEST!
GIRL'S GLEE
O
MRS. PITRE
RACIAL PREJUDICED
GERMAN
OOO
MR. ZILLHAUS
SPITS WHEN HE TALKS AND IT LANDS ON YOU.
HOME EC
O
MISS KELLEN
FIRST ASSIGNMENT MAKE UGLY TOTE-BAG, THEN UGLY BLOUSE

PERSONAL INFORMATION: BIRTHDAY: JAN 6TH.
SIGN: CAPRICORN = FASCINATING, SENSUOUS, CAN
GET E.S.P. HOBBIES: ART, POETRY, GUM WRAPPER
CHAIN (ALREADY LONGEST OF ANYONE: 13½ FEET)
FAVORITE COLOR: TURQUOISE. FAVORITE SONG OF ALL:
OOH CHILD OR CRYSTAL BLUE PERSUASION.
BEST FEATURE: CAN GROW LONG NAILS
MAIN DEFECT: NOSE, LIPS, GLASSES, MY WHOLE
FACE AND ENTIRE BODY.

NO WAY AM I CUTER THAN YOU! YOU'RE WAY CUTER!

CUTER HAIR, FOR ONE.

NUH-UH. YOUR HAIR'S CUTER. MINE SPAZMOTIC

WORST THINGS ABOUT MY LIFE RIGHT NOW:
① HAVING LOYCIE WATFORD FOR A LOCKER
PARTNER AND NO ONE WILL TRADE!!!
② LISA MORRIS WANTS TO KICK MY ASS FOR
ACCIDENTLY SPLASHING WATER ON HER NEW
SUEDE BOOTS. I SAID I WAS SORRY BUT DOES
THAT MATTER TO HER?? NO!

MY MAIN GOAL OF LIFE: END POLLUTION,
PREJUDICE AND THE POPULATION EXPLOSION!!!!
I WILL WRITE POEMS PLUS MAKE POSTERS!!!!!

THE TITLE OF IT IS "BECAUSE... POLLUTION IS UNGENTLE AND SMOKESTACKS SUCK (OUR AIR)

READY?

UGLIFUL

BY LYNDA BARRY ©1989

THE FIRST THING ABOUT MY MOM IS THAT SHE WAS VERY BEAUTIFUL WHEN SHE WAS YOUNG. IN FACT, GORGEOUS. THE GORGEOUS TWIN OF AVA GARDNER, EVERYBODY SAID IT. MY MOM HAS TOLD US THIS 10,000 TIMES.

AND DID YOU KNOW I HAD WHAT THEY CONSIDERED PERFECT EYEBROWS?

WELL, IT'S ALL GONE TO HELL NOW. WASTED. SHOWS YOU WHAT HAVING KIDS CAN DO TO YOU.

SHE WAS SO BEAUTIFUL, FIVE GUYS ASKED HER TO MARRY THEM BEFORE SHE PICKED MY FATHER, THE WORST MISTAKE OF HER LIFE. I ALWAYS WONDER WHAT I COULD HAVE LOOKED LIKE INSTEAD, IF SHE HAD PICKED ONE OF THEM.

HERMAN KOSARSKI LOOKED LIKE PERRY COMO

DAVID R. GAVLAK NOW OWNS "GAVLAK SANITATION"

PETER FERRARA BOY COULD HE DANCE.

WAYNE SHIPLEY LOOKED LIKE "MAVERICK"

WILBERT BRUTOUT NOW OWNS "BRUTOUT TEXACO"

8

WHEN I WAS LITTLE, I LOOKED JUST LIKE HER. WE HAD THOSE DRESSES THAT MATCH AND ACCORDING TO MY MOTHER, THE PEOPLE WHO SAW US SAID WE WERE WONDERFUL. THEN I HAD TO GET GLASSES WHICH MY MOTHER HATED BECAUSE IT SPOILED MY LOOKS. THIS WAS A LONG TIME AGO WHEN MY MOM'S EYES WERE PERFECT AND MY DAD WAS STILL WITH US.

MY BABY SISTER MARLYS WHO MY MOM SAYS WAS BORN WEARING GLASSES. AND ALSO "CHUBBY"

"YOU GOT YOUR FATHER'S LOOKS. THE BOTH OF YOU." SHE SAYS TO ME AND MY SISTER WHEN SHE GETS IN THAT ONE TALKING MOOD ABOUT HER MISTAKES IN LIFE. AND SHE TELLS ME I HAD BETTER GET BUSY WORKING ON MY CHARM. "WELL, BE GRATEFUL YOU DON'T HAVE A WEIGHT PROBLEM." SHE SAYS, THEN LOOKS STRAIGHT AT MY SISTER.

9

PERFECT ART

BY LYNDA BARRY and RICK KOT ©1988

I HAVE A COUSIN, RICKY DAVIS, WHO IS MY SAME AGE BUT GOES TO CATHOLIC SCHOOL, ST. GEORGES. HE IS AN INCREDIBLE ARTIST. YOU SHOULD SEE HIS NOSES. THEY ARE SO REALISTIC.

HE DID THIS ONE ASSIGNMENT OF: DRAW THE VIRGIN MARY, RIGHT? HE COPIED THE FACE FROM PAULA PRENTISS. IT WAS SO PERFECT. THE EYES. HE SAID THAT'S HOW YOU CAN TELL PERFECT ART: DO THE EYES LOOK LIKE THEY ARE WATCHING YOU?

GOD. THIS IS SO GOOD. MAN.

THANKS.

NO, SERIOUSLY.

AFTER ONE SECOND OF LOOKING AT IT, ALL YOU COULD THINK WAS: <u>AUTOMATIC A</u>. HE TAPED ON SARAN WRAP AND TURNED IT IN. IF YOU CAN BELIEVE IT, HE GOT IT BACK WITH THE FACE CROSSED OFF. HIS NUN WROTE: "THE VIRGIN MARY IS NOT A BEAUTY QUEEN."

AT FIRST HE WOULDN'T EVEN SHOW ME. FINALLY HE SAID "OK. OPEN THAT DRAWER." I NEVER FORGOT THE FEELING OF BE-FORE AND AFTER WHEN I SAW IT. I NEVER KNEW LOOKING AT A PICTURE COULD MAKE YOU FEEL SO SAD.

11

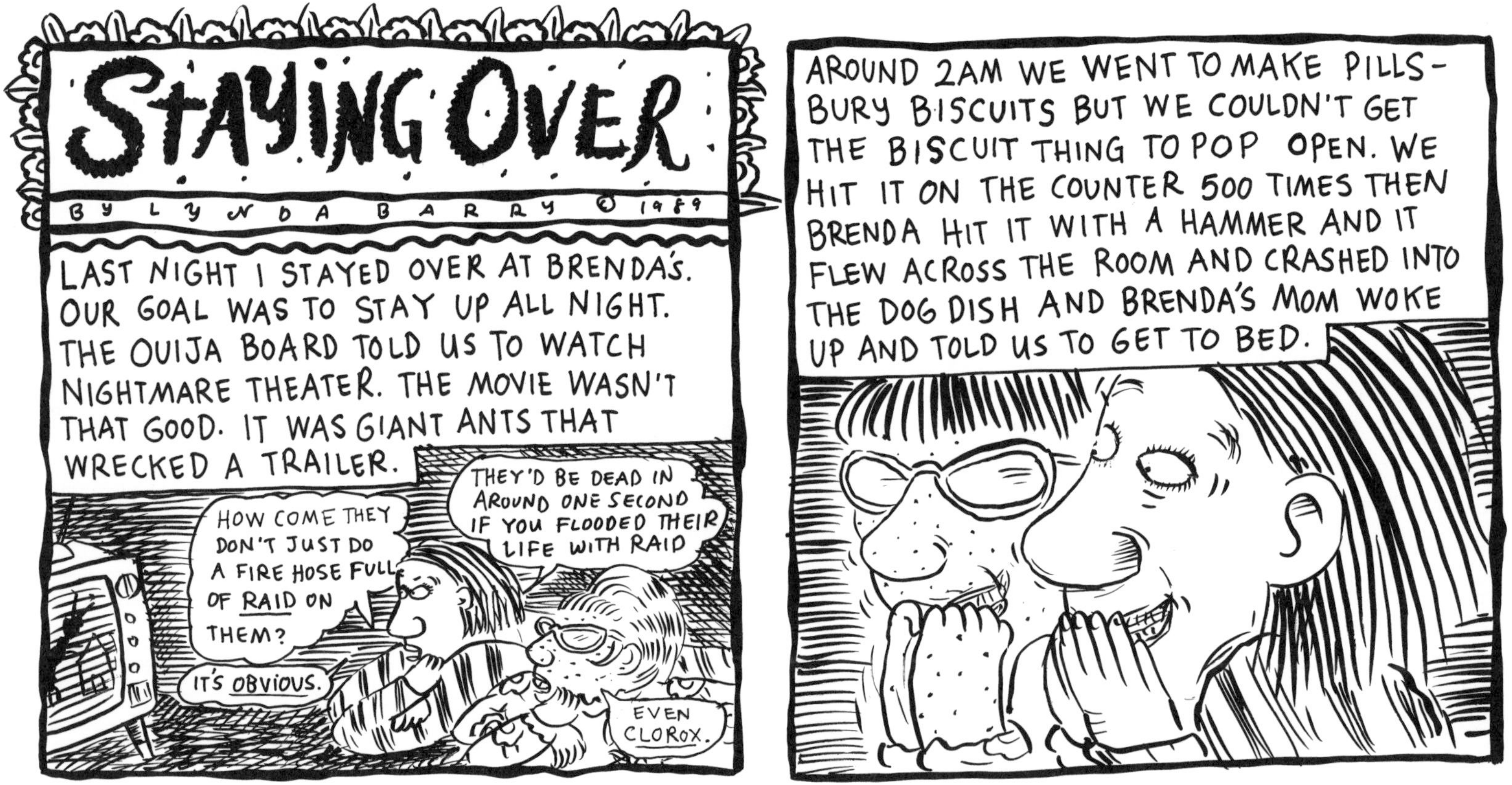
STAYING OVER
BY LYNDA BARRY © 1989
LAST NIGHT I STAYED OVER AT BRENDA'S. OUR GOAL WAS TO STAY UP ALL NIGHT. THE OUIJA BOARD TOLD US TO WATCH NIGHTMARE THEATER. THE MOVIE WASN'T THAT GOOD. IT WAS GIANT ANTS THAT WRECKED A TRAILER.
HOW COME THEY DON'T JUST DO A FIRE HOSE FULL OF RAID ON THEM?
THEY'D BE DEAD IN AROUND ONE SECOND IF YOU FLOODED THEIR LIFE WITH RAID
IT'S OBVIOUS.
EVEN CLOROX.
AROUND 2AM WE WENT TO MAKE PILLS-BURY BISCUITS BUT WE COULDN'T GET THE BISCUIT THING TO POP OPEN. WE HIT IT ON THE COUNTER 500 TIMES THEN BRENDA HIT IT WITH A HAMMER AND IT FLEW ACROSS THE ROOM AND CRASHED INTO THE DOG DISH AND BRENDA'S MOM WOKE UP AND TOLD US TO GET TO BED.

THEN THE GUY ON K.O.L. SAID CALL IN YOUR REQUEST SO WE SNUCK BACK IN THE KITCHEN AND BRENDA REQUESTED A SONG BY CREAM THAT SHE DIDN'T KNOW THE NAME OF ABOUT THE LOVE THAT YOU LAID ON MY TABLE. "IT'S FOR DONNY." SHE SAID. "MAKE IT FROM BRENDA TO DONNY." THE GUY SAID HE'D PLAY IT.

YOUR NAME'S GARY, RIGHT?

MY FRIEND'S IN LOVE WITH YOU.

ONE SEC! ONE SEC MORE!

SHUT UP!

SERI-OUS-LY!

SHE WANTS TO KNOW YOUR ASTROLOGY.

FOR AROUND 3 HOURS HE DIDN'T PLAY THE SONG. WHEN FINALLY IT CAME ON, HE LEFT OUT THE DONNY PART. BRENDA GAVE THE FINGER TO THE RADIO FOR AROUND ONE HALF HOUR AFTER THAT. THEN SHE ASKED ME IF I DARED HER TO CALL HIM UP AND SAY "YOU SUCK" AND ALSO DID I WANT TO MAKE SOME PANCAKES. AND THEN WE STARTED TO HEAR THE BIRDS, 10,000 BIRDS. AND THE LIGHT IN HER ROOM TURNED PALE PALE BLUE.

FLATNESS

BY LYNDA BARRY © 1989 × × × × ×

I LIKE THIS ONE GUY IN MATH. KENNY PAY-TELL. HE'S NOTHING THAT BIG. JUST A GUY WITH GLASSES, ½ SMART AND ½ CORNY ½ CUTE AND ½ FISH FACE.

I LIKE HIM BECAUSE I'M HALF AND HALF TOO, THE SAME WAY. EXCEPT IF YOU'RE A GIRL, FOR "FISH FACE" YOU WRITE "DOG." I LIKE HIM BECAUSE WE HAVE PERFECTLY MATCHING DEFECTS.

BUT IT TURNS OUT THAT KENNY HAS NE-VER FACED REALITY ABOUT THIS BE-CAUSE HE GOES AFTER CHERYL HOLT WHO IS JUST AS DEFECTIVE BUT MAJORLY STACKED. STACKEDNESS EQUALS MINUS FIVE DEFECTS SO COMPARED TO HER, KENNY IS TOO LAME.

BUT BECAUSE OF MY FLATNESS, TO KEN-NY I AM TOO LAME. BECAUSE OF MY FLATNESS, I'M SUPPOSED TO GO WITH A GUY MORE DEFECTIVE THAN ME WHICH THERE IS NO WAY I WILL DO.
IF I PUT JUST A LITTLE MORE KLEENEX IN EVERY DAY, I WONDER WOULD ANYONE NOTICE.

15

BEYOND the EARTH

BY LYNDA BARRY ©89

If you could visit another planet, where would you like to go? Let us pretend to take a long, long trip through space.

VISIT! THE! PLANET! OF! MARLYS!!!!!!

The Planet of Marlys

Sun! mercury! venus! EARTH!

Facts about the Planet of Marlys!
- It has Oxygen!
- How many moons? 58!
- Hardly no Gravity!
- Free CANDY FOR My Friends!

NEWS SPECIAL BULLETIN! Astronauts have discovered the gorgeous planet of MARLYS! They thought that Earth was #1 now theres a tie of which is the best planet! Now they're Voting on Marlys!

Here YE HERE YE!

STOP TALKING!

Please raise your hand who votes MARLYS.

THAT'S 1,000,000,000,000 Votes.

now who is voting earth?

2 votes.

Planet Marlys is obviously the winner

yea!

yea!

The planet Marlys has incredible decorations and rides. It rotates quickly and the people of Marlys are good, they only want peace. Everythings free. For energy they use special dirt. The cars can run on dirt and you can cook with dirt. Also you feel like you are floating.

On the planet Marlys anyone named Marlys is #1 But no Marlys starts acting all conceited Because of it. They have the Marlys parade and the main marlys rides a float. If you want to go to planet Marlys you will just have to wait for the future! In the future you can come to planet Marlys!!!! It will be great!!!

ON TUESDAY

BY LYNDA BARRY ✿✿✿✿✿✿✿✿ © 1988

MY SISTER MARLYS ANSWERED THE PHONE AND THEN YELLED THROUGH MY DOOR "IT'S BRIAN BANO!" AND AT FIRST I ALMOST DIDN'T UNLOCK IT BECAUSE I THOUGHT SHE WAS LYING. YOU KNOW HIM? HE'S IN NINTH. A NINTH GRADER.

YOU SWEAR TO GOD?

WHY. IS HE SOME KIND OF BIG DEAL?

I SPENT MY WHOLE PHONE LIMIT ON HIM. ONE HOUR OF TALKING ON MY MOM'S BED WITH ALL THE LIGHTS OFF AND THE UNIVERSE FEELING PERFECT. THEN HE CALLED ME FOR AROUND 9 STRAIGHT NIGHTS AND I WAS WONDERING: DOES IT EQUAL HE IS MY BOYFRIEND?

OH, I DON'T KNOW. YEAH. SORT OF. WHY? DO YOU? REALLY? SERIOUSLY? UH-HUH. YEAH.

NO! NO WAY! YOU DO? SAME HERE. YEAH.

18

THEN HE SAID DID I WANT TO SKIP WITH HIM ON TUESDAY AND MEET UP AT CROFTON PARK. THERE'S SOME PLACES HE KNOWS OF WHERE YOU CAN GET YOUR PRIVACY. I DIDN'T KNOW IF IT WAS ONE OF THOSE THINGS WHERE IF YOU SAY NO, THEY QUIT LIKING YOU, SO EVEN THOUGH I FELT ONLY HALF AND HALF, I SAID OK.

HI.

HI.

AFTERWARDS, WALKING HOME, I KEPT FEELING LIKE WHOEVER EVEN LOOKED AT ME COULD TELL WHAT I JUST DID. I MADE A HOLY VOW 100 TIMES OF: NO WAY NEVER AGAIN. THEN FOR 11 DAYS HE DIDN'T CALL AND DIDN'T CALL, AND I KEPT THINKING ABOUT HIM MORE AND MORE AND NOW THE PHONE JUST RANG, HIM SAYING MEET ME UP AT CROFTON PARK IN ONE HOUR AND I DON'T KNOW. I GUESS I'M GOING.

19

CHOREOGRAPHY
LYNDA BARRY ©1989
Choreography Outline
Maybonne
P.E., Miss Hundley 2nd
GROUP 2: Brenda, Denise, Renee, Vicky, Mayb
CONCEPT: Evolution, then the earth blows up
Music: "Black Magic Woman"
I. Beginning Action: When the music starts, we are spores in a circle.
PSSST.
WHAT?
DO YOU FEEL LIKE A SPAZ?
II. Slow motion: We start to grow. We are amazed by our new life. It's amazing to us. We love our new life. there's expressions of amazement, and there's discovery
Movements: mainly spinning
PLEASE, GOD. DON'T LET HER PICK OURS FOR THE ASSEMBLY. I BEG YOU.

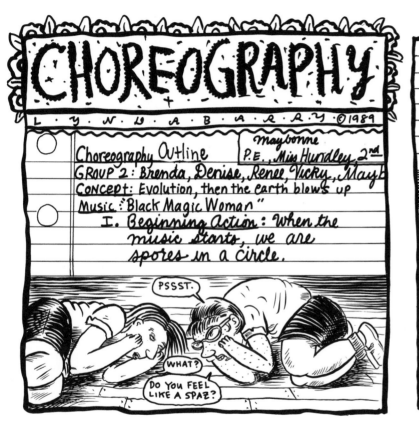

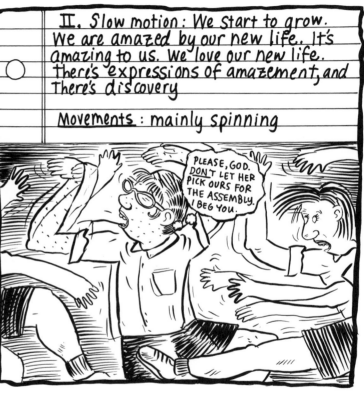

III. The music goes fast. It starts symbolizing civilization, man, violence, war, pollution. We get horrified. We can't even look. We keep running but cannot escape. Then we fall and it's like there's acid pouring on us.

MOVEMENTS: reaching, running, pivots, rolls

IV. Resolution: We're rolling then suddenly we stop and you think we are dead. Suddenly you realize it's that Spore Thing.

Ending Action: At the end of the music Vicky reaches one arm up and makes her face like "why? why? why?"

Message: It's an eternal cycle

ON THURSDAY

BY LYNDA BARRY ❀❀❀❀❀❀❀ ©1988.

This class SUCKS!!

I know. I am so bored

LOOK at Mrs. Lahaye's armpits

Aren't you glad you use dial?
Don't you wish everybody did?

Do you know whats for lunch?

I think chili

IS It true about you and Brian Bano?

what?

CROFTON PARK and all that.
No. who said?
DEB BARTLEtt who else?
What did she say?
YOU HAD A MAKE OUT SESSION
Im sure! How should she know about my life?
HER LITTLE SISTER KNOWS YOUR LITTLE SISTER
I don't get it.
Your sister read your diary and told her.
Marlys?
Is it true?
I don't even have a diary.
Deb Bartlett told the story of it on the bus.
Shes such a liar!
It sounded realistic.
100% *NO WAY!!!!!!!!!*
Brian Banos cute. I wouldn't mind it.
Come off it!
Are you Being for real? Please tell me!
As if I would even have to lie!
Then you Better get Deb Bartlett for it at lunch
because she is spreading it to the
whole universe.

There is just no way!
better act cool or we are gonna get busted.

Its not true.
OK.

Do You know what you are Doing
your report on yet?
            No.
Do DESEASES OF PLANTS WITH me.
Maybe.

Are you mad at me?
       No.

Do you even like Brian Bano?

       No.

JANUARY 4th

L Y N D A B A R R Y © 1989

Marlys STOP READING THIS!!! PRIVATE!!!
Dear Diary. It's hard to write because I got the flu and everything looks freaked out. I got it in Math. Mr. Ruppert thought I was faking but I went to the nurse and my fever was 101°. They called up Mom to get me.

I about gave Mr. Ruppert the finger. I had to lay down on this couch thing with a blanket on me by the teachers lounge. They smoked about a million cigarettes. and Mr. Zillhaus told a stupid joke I swear to god about a guy's dinger and everyone was laughing. Then I konked out. And then when I opened my eyes this ninth grader, Warren Eng, was sitting across from me with a blanket wrapped on him for the same thing. He said hi then I said hi then he threw up. It was embarrassing. It was in the garbage can. In a way I was freaking out because after that I about threw up too. Then we started talking. Turns out he thinks Mr. Ruppert sucks also. Our moms came, then in the parking lot he waved me good bye and then I waved back then Mom said now don't tell me you have a Chinese Boyfriend. Right Mom. But truthfully I never noticed how cute Warren Eng is before. And if a certain person is reading this I will demolish her.

MOM SAYS FOR ME TO ASK YOU CAN YOU EAT DINNER WITHOUT BARFING YET AND WHO EVEN CARES ABOUT YOUR STUPID DIARY?

JANUARY 18TH

L Y N D A   B A R R Y   © 1 9 8 9

Brian Bono doesn't like me anymore and I don't even know why. He won't even talk to me. I heard he's calling up Debbie Becker. I feel so messed up by it I can't even blink my eyes. Staring staring staring staring

My stupid sister just came in and told <s>my</s> me dinner. How am I even supposed to eat. Moms going to yell at me for not being cheerful. I'm sorry mom but its around my worst day of life so far.

HEY. HOW COME YOU'RE ALREADY IN YOUR PAJAMAS?

HUH?

HUH?

O.K. WHO CARES.

BE A SNOB.

I just came from dinner. Mom didn't say anything to me. Her and marlys talked. She didn't say anything about me hardly eating. I tried calling up Sharon but she's on phone restriction and her dad was cold to me. The whole world hates me.

HEY WANT SOME SEVEN-UP? I'LL GET YOU SOME SEVEN-UP.

THERES SOME CHEF-BOY-AR-DEE LEFT. WANT SOME OF THAT?

WANT TO HEAR A JOKE?

I just called up Brian's house which his mom answered. She told me girls shouldn't call boys up then she said Brian and then he said hello then I said hello then he said who is this and I said Maybonne then he said he had to go. I don't even know what I did. I don't even know what I did to make him stop liking me. Please at least tell me what I did.

DO YOU WANT ME TO STAY IN HERE OR FLAKE OFF? I'LL FLAKE OFF IF YOU WANT. HAVE THIS 7UP. SHOULD I CALL MOM?

The Famous Bee

BY LYNDA BARRY ©89

TODAY THERE WAS A GIGANTOR BEE FLYING IN MATH WHICH WAS WEIRD BECAUSE HOW MANY BEES DO YOU KNOW FLYING IN JANUARY? MR. RUPPERT SAID HE REFUSED TO HAVE HIS CLASS DISRUPTED BY AN INSECT SO IGNORE IT. THEN IT LANDED ON THE BOARD AND STARTED CRAWLING ON THE PROBLEMS.

WHEN IT TOOK OFF AND LANDED ON ROBERT DELGARDO'S DESK, HE RAISED HIS HAND FOR IF HE SHOULD KILL IT WITH HIS MATH BOOK AND MR. RUPPERT SLAMMED HIS FIST DOWN AND SAID "WHAT DID I JUST SAY, ROBERT?" AND THEN THE BEE FLEW UP ONTO ONE OF THE LIGHTS AND STARTED WALKING AROUND IT IN A CIRCLE.

28

FOR AROUND TEN MINUTES THAT IS ALL IT DID AND NO ONE COULD HELP WATCHING IT UNTIL MR. RUPPERT YELLED "OK, IF YOU THINK WATCHING THAT GOD DAMN BEE IS MORE INTERESTING THAN MATH, THAT IS WHAT WE WILL DO." AND WE ALL HAD TO LOOK UP AND WATCH THE BEE WHICH BY NOW WASN'T MOVING.

WE STARED AT THE BEE FOR AROUND SEVEN MINUTES STRAIGHT WHILE MR. RUPPERT SAT AT HIS DESK CORRECTING PAPERS AND ASKING US IF WE WERE ENJOYING THE SHOW. THEN ALL OF A SUDDEN THE BEE DROPPED OFF THE LIGHT AND THE WHOLE CLASS SCREAMED INCLUDING MR. RUPPERT WHO IT TURNS OUT IS KIND OF JUMPY.

FEB 23 DEAR DIARY

BY LINDA BARRY

TODAY ME AND BRENDA BOTH HAD TO BABYSIT SO BRENDA SAID JUST BRING OVER MARLYS AND BABYSIT HER HERE AND MARLYS SAID NO BECAUSE SHE HATES BRENDA'S BROTHER ROLAND SO I HAD TO PAY MARLYS 25¢, THE SCROUNGE.

HI.

HI.

SHUT-UP.

YOU SHUT-UP

IT'S MY HOUSE.

YOU STILL HAVE TO SHUT UP.

FOR LUNCH WE WERE GOING TO MAKE M+M PANCAKES EXCEPT ROLAND RIPPED US OFF OF OUR M+Ms WHICH WE BOUGHT WITH OUR OWN MONEY, THEN BRENDA GOT MAD, AND HE TOLD HER TO BITE IT, THEN SHE THREW A PLATE AND IT BASHED BY HIS HEAD.

KRASH

THEN ROLAND SOCKED HER STOMACH AND RAN OUTSIDE THEN BRENDA STARTS CRYING AND YELLING SHE HATES EVERYTHING AND GOES IN HER MOM'S ROOM AND SLAMS THE DOOR THEN MARLYS SAYS SHE'S LEAVING AND I TELL HER NO BUT SHE DOES ANYWAY, THEN BRENDA COMES OUT AND TOLD ME THAT HER WHOLE LIFE SUCKS.

WAIT 'TIL I TELL MOM. YOU'RE IN TROUBLE FOR EVEN TAKING ME HERE, MAN.

SHE SAID SHE WAS DEPRESSED ON THE CRUDDINESS OF HER LIFE AND NO BOYS LIKING HER AND SHE WANTED TO COMMIT SUICIDE. THEN I TOLD HER I FELT THAT EXACT SAME WAY AFTER BRIAN BANO AND THEN I SAID "YOU'VE GOT A FRIEND" TO HER, THEN SHE STARTED CRYING THEN I STARTED CRYING BECAUSE EVEN THOUGH LIFE DOES SUCK, SOMETIMES IT CAN ALSO BE BEAUTIFUL.

CLEANLINESS

By LYNN BARRY '89

I HAVE THIS THING WHERE I CAN'T SLEEP. I CAN HEAR MY MOM WALKING IN THE KITCHEN. SHE CAN'T SLEEP EITHER. I TRY TO SLEEP BUT MY CLOCK RADIO JUST KEEPS GOING: 2:00, 3:00, 4:00. RIGHT NOW I THINK SHE'S MOPPING.

LAST NIGHT AT 3:37 AM, SHE STARTED RUNNING THE VACUUM. IT WOKE UP MY SISTER. "GO BACK TO BED" MOM TOLD HER. "YOU'RE YOUNG. YOU CAN SLEEP THROUGH ANYTHING." MARLYS TOLD ME SHE RAN DOWNSTAIRS BECAUSE SHE THOUGHT IT WAS THE ATOM BOMB.

MOM GETS LIKE THIS. WHEN OUR DAD LEFT, OUR HOUSE SMELLED LIKE LYSOL FOR A YEAR. 4:02 AM. I CAN HEAR THE COFFEE POT. IT HAS THE SOUND OF ASTHMA. THE SADDEST BREATHING IN THE WORLD. SHE'S DOING SOMETHING WITH THE STOVE. SHE CLEANED THE STOVE LAST NIGHT. I WONDER IF SHE FORGOT. I CAN SMELL HER CIGARETTE. I WONDER IF I LIT ONE COULD SHE TELL.

4:07 AM. THE BATHROOM LIGHT GOES ON. MARLYS. IT GOES OFF AND SHE COMES IN MY ROOM. "YOU'RE SMOKING" SHE SAYS AND YAWNS. SHE SITS ON MY BED. "I CAN'T SLEEP" SHE SAYS. WE CAN SMELL THE OVEN CLEANER SPRAYING DOWN-STAIRS. "IT'S JUST YOUR IMAGINATION" I TELL HER.

MY PERFECT LIFE

BY LYNDA BARRY © 1989

WE WERE EATING DINNER AND THE DOORBELL RINGS AND IT'S BRENDA AND SHE'S CRYING AND SHE HAS TO TALK TO ME AND MY MOM SAYS NO BECAUSE: #1 WE ARE EATING, #2 SHE DIDN'T CALL FIRST, #3 MY MOM IS TOTAL JIVE!!!

I SAID PLEASE MOM. JUST FOR ONE SECOND SO I CAN SEE WHAT'S THE PROBLEM AND MY MOM SAYS ARE YOU BRENDA'S PSYCHIATRIST? THEN I SAY MOM YOU ARE SO COLD BLOODED AND THEN MARLYS KICKS ME TO MAKE ME SHUT UP SO I KICK HER BACK ACCIDENTLY TOO HARD AND SHE STARTS CRYING SO I GET RESTRICTION, ONE WEEK!

OBVIOUSLY MY APPITITE IS GOING TO BE
WRECKED BY THAT BUT MY MOM SAYS <u>EAT</u>
THEN THE PHONE RINGS AND IT'S BRENDA
BUT MY MOM SAYS NO I CAN'T TALK TO HER
SO I SAY THIS IS A CONCENTRATION CAMP
THEN I GET RESTRICTION TWO WEEKS AND
I STILL DON'T KNOW WHAT IS WRONG
WITH BRENDA.

I BEGGED MARLYS JUST PLEASE CALL BRENDA
AND ASK HER WHAT'S WRONG BUT MARLYS
SAYS I MUST BE HIGH IF I THINK SHE WILL
DO <u>ANYTHING</u> FOR ME. SO NOW MY SISTER
HATES ME, MY MOM HATES ME, AND MY BEST
FRIEND MAYBE MIGHT COMMIT SUICIDE. I MEAN,
I WAS JUST SITTING THERE AND SUDDENLY
MY WHOLE LIFE GOT RUINED!

WHAT HAPPENED?

BY LYNDA BARRY ©89

I AM ON TOTAL RESTRICTION FOR NOTHING.!!! SO I CAN'T TALK TO BRENDA! SO MARLYS COMES IN MY ROOM AND SAYS "OK I GOT THE REASON FROM BRENDA ABOUT WHY SHE CAME OVER HERE CRYING YESTERDAY. I CALLED HER UP FOR YOU."

TELL ME.

WE BETTER SHUT THE DOOR.

MARLYS SAID THE STORY OF IT AND IT WEIRDED ME OUT! IT WOULD WEIRD ANYBODY OUT! BUT I BET THE MOST WEIRDED OUT WAS BRENDA!!!

OK. SHE SAID HER LIFE IS RUINED BECAUSE THAT GUY JIM IN MATH, SHE WENT OVER TO HIS BASEMENT, AND HE THOUGHT HE WAS COOL BY PLAYING A DRUM SOLO, THEN HE KISSED HER AND AUTOMATICALLY DID A FRENCH AND TRIED TO DO A F.U. AND AN ELVIS ON HER. THEN A DOOR OPENS.

AND IT WAS HIS MOM AND SHE HAD ON AN UGLY WIG AND SHE YELLED AT BRENDA GET OUT!

36

MARLYS ASKED ME WHAT WAS A FRENCH, A F.U. AND AN ELVIS AND I SAID THAT I DIDN'T KNOW AND SHE SAID WHAT A LIAR, BUT WHAT WAS I SUPPOSED TO SAY?! LIKE I'M GOING TO TELL HER!!! LIKE I'M GOING TO MESS UP MY SISTER'S MIND!! THEN MARLYS SAID FOR ME TO FORGET ABOUT HER TELLING ME THE REST OF WHAT HAPPENED TO BRENDA! IS THAT ANY FAIR??!! NO!!

THEN THERE'S A NOISE ON THE WINDOW AND I LOOK AND IT'S BRENDA AND SHE'S CRYING AND MARLYS SAYS "I'M TELLING MOM UNLESS I CAN STAY IN HERE. IF YOU LET HER IN AND TRY TO MAKE ME GO, I'M GOING TO BUST YOU TO MOM." IT WAS SO COLD OF MARLYS! SO I SAID OK, AND THAT I HATED HER GUTS, AND THEN I OPENED THE WINDOW AND LET BRENDA IN.

THE WORST NEWS

BY LYNDA BARRY © 1989 X OO XX O

BRENDA IS RUNNING AWAY. IT IS FOR REAL. SHE SNUCK IN MY BEDROOM WINDOW AND TOLD ME HER LIFE WAS DEMOLISHED. THE DISTURBED AUNT IS COMING TO LIVE WITH THEM PERMA-NANTLY.

CAN YOU SEE ME HAVING PEOPLE OVER?

LIKE "HI. THIS IS MY CRAZY AUNT"

WE GOT A CRAZY UNCLE.

CAN I HOLD YOUR CIGARETTE?

NO.

MAN! YOU NEVER LET ME DO ANYTHING! I HATE YOU!

SHUT UP MARLYS.

HER NAME IS AUNT EINA. I ALREADY MET HER LAST SUMMER. SHE TOLD ME AND BRENDA THAT SHE WAS NOT CRAZY, ONLY THAT A MAN LIVED IN HER STOMACH. THE MAIN WEIRD THING ABOUT HER IS SHE SAYS "GET OUT OF MY BELLY" OVER AND OVER.

I'D LET YOU HOLD MY CIGARETTE.

IT IS SUCKY, BUT DON'T RUN AWAY!

ALREADY TOO LATE. I LEFT A NOTE FOR MY MOM.

IT TURNS OUT AUNT EINA IS GOING TO GET BRENDA'S ROOM AND BRENDA IS SUPPOSED TO SHARE A ROOM WITH HER BROTHER ROLAND!!!!! WHEN MARLYS HEARS THAT PART, SHE MAKES THE SOUND OF BARFING.

THEN I HEAR THE PHONE RINGING AND MY MOM YELLS IT'S BRENDA'S MOM, DO I KNOW WHERE BRENDA IS AND BRENDA STARTS CLIMBING OUT THE WINDOW SAYING "DON'T BUST ME" AND I SAY "WAIT" AND MY MOM YELLS MY NAME AND I YELL "IN A SEC!" THEN MOM OPENS MY DOOR AND I JUST STAND THERE AS NORMAL AS POSSIBLE.

WHICH WAY?

BY LYNDA BARRY © 1 9 8 9 × × × ×

MY BEST FRIEND BRENDA RAN AWAY AND
HER MOM, MRS. BILOW, CAME OVER CRYING WITH
THE POLICE WHO TALKED TO ME ABOUT THE
SERIOUSNESS AND I TOLD THEM THE TRUTH.
THAT I DIDN'T KNOW WHERE SHE WENT.

THEN MY SISTER MARLYS TOLD THEM THE
OTHER TRUTH OF BRENDA SNEAKING IN MY
WINDOW AND SMOKING TWO CIGARETTES AND
TELLING US THE PROBLEMS OF HER LIFE,
THEN CLIMBING OUT AND RUNNING DOWN
THE STREET TOWARD COYLE. THEN THE
POLICE WENT WHEN?! WHEN?! WHAT TIME?!
AND ASKED US TO SAY EVERYTHING SHE
WAS WEARING.

MY MOM PUT HER ARM AROUND MRS. BILOW AND SAID IF I WAS INVOLVED IN THIS, SHE WAS GOING TO SKIN ME ALIVE. THEN THE POLICE ASKED ME AROUND 900 QUESTIONS ABOUT BRENDA'S PERSONAL LIFE. DID SHE TAKE DRUGS, DID SHE HAVE A BOYFRIEND, ALL THAT. AND THEY SAID IF I LIED, I WAS GOING TO JUVINILE.

THEN I COULDN'T HELP IT AND I JUST STARTED CRYING. WHAT WAS I SUPPOSED TO DO WITH NO ONE BELIEVING ME AND THEM ALL ACTING SO COLD BLOODED? I JUST KEPT THINKING IT'S A LUCKY THING FOR THEM I DON'T KNOW WHERE SHE IS. IT'S A LUCKY THING BECAUSE IF I DID, I WOULD NEVER TELL THEM IN A MILLION YEARS.

41

THAT SUCKS!

BY LYNDA BARRY © 1989

MY MOM JUST TOLD ME MRS. BILOW CALLED AND THEY FOUND BRENDA AND SHE IS OK. I TRIED GETTING MORE DETAILS BUT MOM KEPT YELLING ABOUT WHAT SHE WOULD DO IF I TRIED RUNNING AWAY. I GET YELLED AT FOR SOMETHING I NEVER EVEN DID YET!

YOU JUST NEVER MIND WHERE SHE WAS!

BY GOD IF YOU PULL A STUNT LIKE THAT YOU BETTER HOPE TO GOD I NEVER FIND YOU. I'LL MAKE YOU WISH YOU HAD BLAH BLAH BLAH BLAH

THEN SHE SAYS BRENDA'S A TROUBLE MAKER AND I CAN'T SEE HER ANYMORE. SHE CALLS HER "THAT BRENDA." LIKE MOM CAN MAKE THE RULES ON WHO CAN BE MY FRIEND!! SO I ACCIDENTLY SAY "THAT SUCKS", RIGHT? IS "THAT SUCKS" SWEARING? NO! BUT MOM STARTS SCREAMING AT ME FOR SWEARING AT HER!!! "THAT SUCKS" IS NOT SWEARING!!!!

IT'S JUST A SAYING, MOM!!

WHAT DO YOU THINK I AM? STUPID??

I SWEAR TO GOD!!!

42

THEN MOM STARTS THAT THING OF "MY OWN DAUGHTER, MY OWN DAUGHTER" AND SHE SAYS SHE DOESN'T UNDERSTAND WHAT HAS HAPPENED TO ME! ALL THAT HAS HAPPENED TO ME IS SHE'S GONE CRAZY!!! THEN MY STUPID IDIOT SISTER COMES IN AND I SAY "MARLYS. IS 'THAT SUCKS' SWEARING?" AND MARLYS SAYS YES! IT'S SO OBVIOUS SHE IS JUST TAKING MOM'S SIDE!! I HATE HER!!

SHE'S LYING!!

AM NOT.

MOM, CAN I HAVE 50¢ FOR SOMETHING EDUCATIONAL?

SO I GO UP TO MY ROOM, OK? AND I ACCIDENTLY SLAM THE DOOR. ACCIDENTLY!!! AND MOM COMES RUNNING IN AND SAYS I THINK THE WORLD REVOLVES AROUND ME!! I DON'T EVEN GET WHAT SHE'S TALKING ABOUT!! AND I GOT ANOTHER WEEK OF RESTRICTION FOR NOT DOING ANYTHING!!! THAT SUCKS, MOM! THAT SUCKS THAT SUCKS THAT SUCKS THAT SUCKS ONE MILLION TIMES INTO INFINITY!!!

GET OUT.

IT'S DINNER.

GET OUT!

MOM!! MAYBONNE WON'T COOPERATE!

Diary

43

MY IMAGINATION

L·Y·N·D·A·B·A·R·R·Y   © 1989

EVER SINCE BRENDA GOT BACK FROM RUNNING AWAY SHE'S BEEN WEIRD TO ME. SHE'S BEEN HANGING AROUND SANDY ALFANO MORE AND MORE AND TODAY SHE TOLD ME SHE NEEDED HER LOVE NECKLACE BACK.

I'LL SEE YA, OK.

UH.

OK.

HEY SANDY!

HEY SANDY!

SHE GAVE IT TO ME THE DAY SHE LEFT, TO PROVE WE WERE BEST FRIENDS AND I GAVE HER MY FLOWER RING AND WE CRIED. I DON'T GET WHATS SO BIG ABOUT SANDY. JUST BECAUSE HER DAD OWNS ALFANO'S MEATS AND SHE CAN GET FREE BEEF JERKY. JUST BECAUSE ALL THE BOYS LIKE HER.

WANNA SKIP 4TH WITH ME

HEY SANDY

SANDY GOTS NEW BOOTS

HEY SANDY. NICE BOOTS.

44

YESTERDAY I WAITED FOR BRENDA SO WE COULD WALK HOME BUT IT TURNS OUT SHE WENT WITH SANDY. THEN TODAY IN HOME EC SANDY DUMPED OUT HER PURSE AND I SAW MY FLOWER RING. AT LUNCH I COULDN'T FIND BRENDA UNTIL RIGHT BEFORE THE BELL.

I ASKED HER IS SANDY YOUR NEW BEST FRIEND NOW AND SHE SAID IT WAS JUST MY IMAGINATION. I ASKED HER ABOUT MY FLOWER RING AND SHE SAYS SHE THINKS SHE MIGHT HAVE LOST IT.

IF YOU ARE STILL MY BEST FRIEND

BY LYNDA BARRY ❀ ❀ ❀ ❀ ❀ © 1989

Dear Brenda, I don't get what your deal is and don't say it's my imagination because that's a major lie. Ever since you've been hanging around Sandy you've been acting different. No offense but you are turning plastic like her.

BRENDA. HERE. IT'S PRIVATE.

FAN MAIL FROM SOME FLOUNDER?

YEAH. OK.

LETS READ IT IN THE CAN.

COME ON.

BRENDA

Remember how you said Sandy was stuck up and in love with herself and how you hated her? Then you told me you needed your Love necklace back, then I saw her wearing it. I know it's a free world, but that is weird.

WHAT A LIAR!! I NEVER SAID THAT ABOUT YOU!!

SHE'S LYING!!

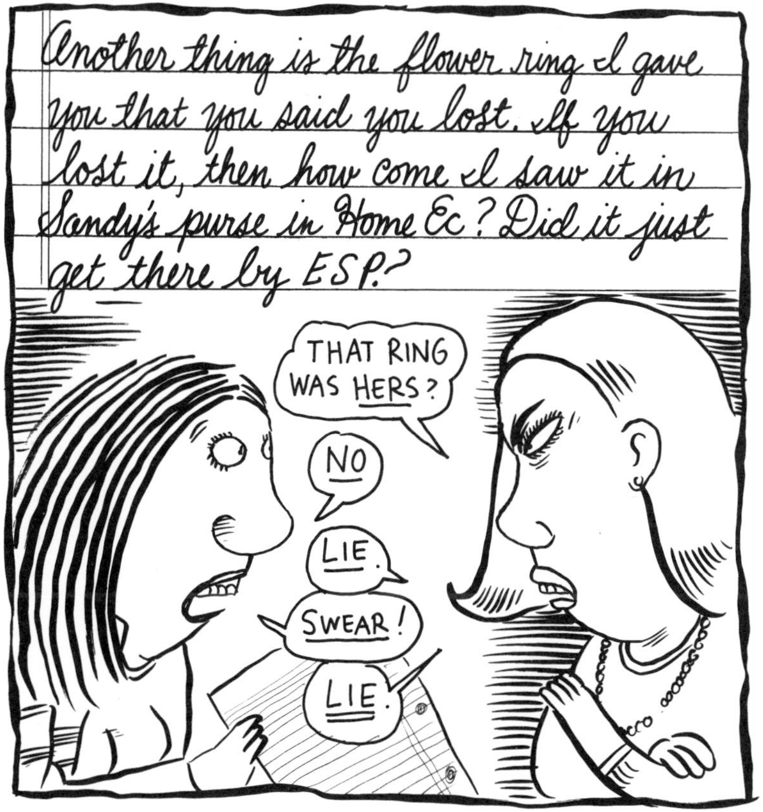
Another thing is the flower ring I gave you that you said you lost. If you lost it, then how come I saw it in Sandy's purse in Home Ec? Did it just get there by ESP?
THAT RING WAS HERS?
NO
LIE
SWEAR!
LIE

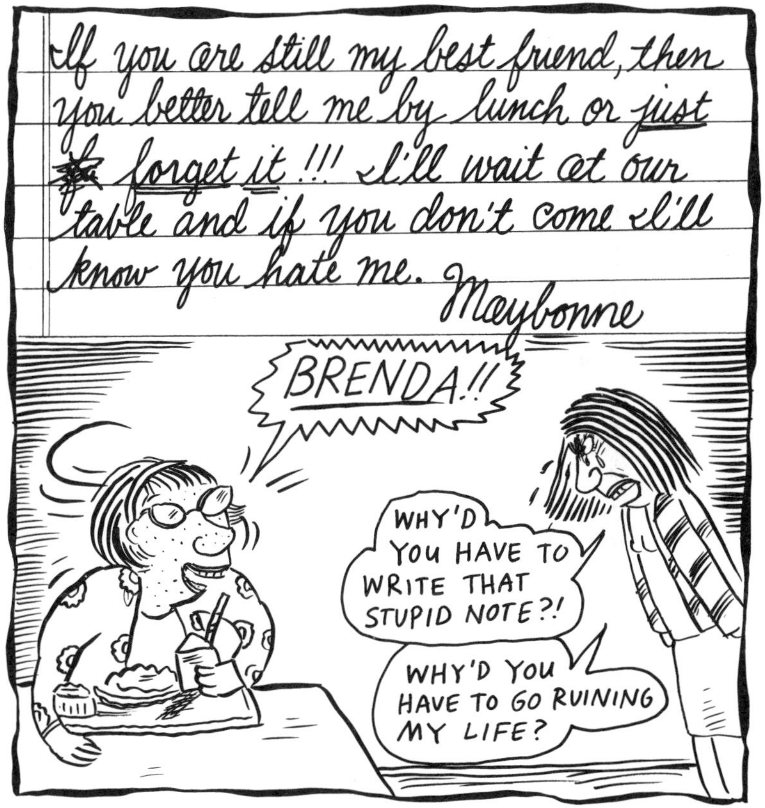
If you are still my best friend, then you better tell me by lunch or just forget it!!! I'll wait at our table and if you don't come I'll know you hate me.
Maybonne
BRENDA!!
WHY'D YOU HAVE TO WRITE THAT STUPID NOTE?!
WHY'D YOU HAVE TO GO RUINING MY LIFE?

ADVICE

by LYNDA BARRY © 1989

YESTERDAY MY COUSIN RICKY CAME OVER AND TOLD ME I LOOKED LIKE I WAS RIDING ON A BUMMER. I TOLD HIM ABOUT MY BEST FRIEND BRENDA TURNING COLD ON ME AND HOW I DIDN'T KNOW WHAT TO DO.

WHATS YOUR ADVICE?

HATE HER.

I DID ALREADY.

GET BACK AT HER.

HE SAID MAKE HER JEALOUS BY GETTING A NEW BEST FRIEND. I SAID YEAH BUT HOW? HE SAID THE MAIN THING IS JUST DON'T ACT TOO HARD UP AND SCROUNGY ABOUT IT. ALSO, DON'T PICK A GIRL THATS TOO STRAIGHT BUT ALSO NOT TOO SCUMMY.

YEAH, BUT WHO?

WE STARTED THINKING OF POSSIBLE NAMES AND THEN I GOT TO CHERYL HOLT. IN SO MANY WAYS SHE IS PERFECT. SHE'S IN HONORS MATH BUT SHE ALSO SMOKES. ALSO WE COULD BE OBVIOUS ABOUT IT BECAUSE HER LOCKER IS RIGHT BY BRENDA'S.

MY ONLY PROBLEM IS THAT I DON'T REALLY LIKE CHERYL HOLT ALL THAT MUCH. I MEAN, SHE'S SLIGHTLY A DUD. BUT FOR RIGHT NOW THAT DOESN'T EVEN MATTER TO ME. FOR RIGHT NOW, ALL I CARE ABOUT IS SHOWING BRENDA HOW STUPID SHE WAS FOR LOSING ME AS A BEST FRIEND.

BEAUTIFUL

BY LYNDA BARRY with IRA GLASS © 1989

YOU KNOW THOSE BIG-EYE PICTURES? CHERYL HOLT HAS 27. ALL HER ALLOWANCE MONEY GOES TO THEM. SHE SAYS THEY ARE HER LIFE.

"IF I COULD HAVE ONE WISH IN LIFE IT WOULD BE TO HAVE MY EYES LIKE THAT."

I ASKED HER "DON'T THEY CREEP YOU OUT IN A WAY? ALL THE EYES?" SHE SAID FOR ME TO EVEN SAY THAT, PROVED I WASN'T DEEP. "IF YOU'RE DEEP" SHE SAID, "THE EYES WILL AUTOMATICALLY MAKE YOU START CRYING."

THAT'S THE MIRACLE OF THEM.

SHE STARED AT THE BALLERINA UNTIL TWO TEARS CAME DOWN. I TRIED STARING AT THE BALLERINA BUT NOTHING HAPPENED. I TRIED IT WITH THE CLOWN, THE HOBO CHILDREN AND THE GARBAGE-CAN-DOG, BUT THE SAME THING.

I WASN'T ABOUT TO HAVE CHERYL TELLING PEOPLE HOW I FLUNKED THE TEST FOR DEEPNESS SO WHEN SHE WASN'T LOOKING, I DRIPPED SOME SPRITE UNDER MY EYES. "CHERYL," I SAID. "LOOK."

THEY'RE BEAUTIFUL

DID I SEE IT?

BY LYNDA BARRY ©89

MY FRIEND CHERYL'S FATHER'S BIG JOKE IS TO SLAP HER PANTS WHEN SHE WALKS BY AND YESTERDAY HE SLAPPED MY PANTS TOO AND THEN LOOKED AT ME WITH A LOOK I STILL CAN'T STOP SEEING. HIS YELLOW TEETH AND UGLY EYES.

I TRIED MENTIONING SOME WORDS ABOUT IT TO CHERYL, LIKE "DOESN'T IT BUG YOU?" AND SHE GAVE ME A LOOK, THE COLDEST LOOK OF SHUT UP. "AT LEAST I HAVE A DAD" SHE SAID. A COMMENT ON ME.

52

WE WALKED INTO THE FRONT ROOM AND HE DID IT AGAIN. CHERYL'S MOM GOT UP AND WALKED OUT. WAS SHE WHISPERING "SON OF A BITCH"? WE WERE LAYING ON THE FLOOR, WATCHING TV, HER DAD IN A CHAIR BEHIND US. THEN HE SAT ON THE COUCH AND SAID FOR CHERYL TO SIT ON THE COUCH.

COME SIT WITH ME.

NO, THAT'S OK.

PLEASE

NO, I'M GOOD HERE.

IT FELT WEIRD LAYING THERE ALONE WITH THEM BEHIND ME BUT I ACTED NORMAL UNTIL THE SHOW FINALLY ENDED AND I COULD SAY "I'M GOING." I TURNED AND DID I REALLY SEE IT? HIS HAND NOT SLAPPING BUT DOING A SLOW CIRCLE, AND CHERYL'S EYES STRAIGHT ON THE TV, NOT BLINKING, AND HER MOUTH FROZEN SHUT.

IS·IT·MY·BUSINESS?

BY·L·Y·N·D·A·B·A·R·R·Y·©89

OK. SAY IT WAS TRUE WHAT I SAW. CHERYL'S DAD TOUCHING HER.

SAY IT WAS TRUE AND NOT MY DECREPIT IMAGINATION. THEN WHAT? IS IT EVEN MY BUSINESS? PLEASE GOD, TELL ME.

IF IT WASN'T HER DAD I'D TELL HER "NEXT TIME HE DOES IT, KICK HIM BETWEEN THE LEGS." EVEN DEAR ABBY WOULD GIVE THAT ADVICE. THEN RUN. RUN LIKE CRAZY.

YEAH BUT IF IT'S ALREADY HER FATHER, WHERE IS SHE SUPPOSED TO RUN TO?

MR. RUPPERT

LYNDA BARRY ✿ ✿ ✿ ✿ ✿ ✿ ✿ © 1989

I HEARD MY MATH TEACHER'S VOICE IN LINE AT THE THRIFTWAY SAYING TO THE CASHIER "WELL, YOU'RE STILL IN LUCK, SHEILA. I'M STILL SINGLE." IT WAS HIM, BUYING 4 CHICKEN POT PIES AND A BOX OF VANILLA WAFERS.

SHE PUT HIS STUFF IN THE BAG AND SAID "WELL, OK THEN, SEE YOU." BUT HE KEPT STANDING THERE EVEN AFTER SHE STARTED ON MY MOM BECAUSE, I GUESS, HE LIKED HER. THEN HE STARTED TELLING SOME OF HIS LAME JOKES. THEY WERE THE SAME BAD JOKES AS IN OUR CLASS. IT WAS FREAKING ME OUT SO BAD I HAD TO GO STAND BY THE MAGAZINES.

OK. HERE'S ANOTHER ONE.

I GOT ANOTHER ONE FOR YA.

OH FOR THE LOVE OF GOD. WHO IS HE, MILTON BERLE?

WHEN HE FINALLY LEFT, THE CASHIER LOOKED AT THE DOOR THEN LOOKED AT MY MOM AND SAID "GOD, I HATE IT WHEN HE COMES IN." — I KNOW HE IS CORNEY AND DOOFY IN THAT MATH TEACHER WAY OF UGLY CLOTHES AND DANDRUFF ON HIS GLASSES, BUT WHEN SHE SAID THAT? I FELT LIKE SLUGGING HER.

WELL, TAKES ALL KINDS.

TODAY THE 10TH?

UH-HUH.

THROUGH THE WINDOW I WATCHED MR. RUPPERT GET INTO HIS ORANGE GREMLIN, AND WHEN HE DROVE BY THE FRONT OF THE STORE HE HONKED TWO TIMES AND I SAID TO THE CASHIER "THAT WAS FOR YOU." AND SHE SAID "WHAT WAS, HONEY?"

MOM'S BIRTHDAY

LYNDA BARRY ©1989

IT WAS MARLYS'S IDEA TO GIVE HER A PARTY. I TRIED TO TELL HER MOM DOESN'T WANT A PARTY. ALL SHE WANTS IS A CLEAN HOUSE. BUT MARLYS STARTED MIXING THE BETTY CROCKER AND THE JELLO 1-2-3 ANYWAY.

"YOU DO YOUR THING AND I'LL DO MINE. I AM NOT IN THIS WORLD TO LIVE UP TO YOUR EXPECTATIONS BECAUSE I AM A CHILD OF THE UNIVERSE"

THING SHE HEARD ON THE RADIO

AREN'T EITHER.

AM SO.

FOREMOST MILK

"YOU'LL SEE" MARLYS SAID. "WHEN MOM COMES HOME FROM WORK AND SEES MY GORGEOUS PARTY FOR HER, SHE'S GOING TO FAINT FROM THE AMAZEMENT." THEN SHE BEGGED ME TO TAKE HER TO THE PAY 'N' SAVE SO SHE COULD BUY ALL THE DETAILS. MARLYS SPENT $5.35 OF HER OWN MONEY AND $2.25 OF MINE. ALL I CAN SAY IS SHE BETTER PAY ME BACK.

REACH THAT CARD FOR ME. THE ONE WITH THE DIAMONDS ON IT.

I'M TELLIN' YOU. MOM'S NOT GOING TO PLAY PIN THE TAIL ON THE DONKEY. IT'S A WASTE OF MONEY TO BUY IT.

HOW SHOULD YOU KNOW? YOU DON'T GOT ESP.

58

AT FIVE O'CLOCK, EVERYTHING WAS DONE. AND I HAVE TO ADMIT, IT LOOKED GOOD. I HAVE TO ADMIT EVEN I WAS EXCITED. THERE WAS 32 BALLOONS, GERMAN CHOCOLATE CAKE WITH CANDLES, ORANGE HI-C, THE JELLO DEALS, AND A SIGN: "HAPPY BIRTHDAY MOM" ON A LONG ROW OF PAPER TOWELS THAT LOOKED VERY ARTISTIC.

AND I TURNED OUT TO BE WRONG. SHE DID WANT A PARTY. "YOU KIDS, YOU KIDS" SHE SAID WHEN SHE OPENED THE DOOR, AND SHE PICKED MARLYS UP AND STARTED TO CRY. THEN I STARTED TO CRY. THEN MARLYS STARTED TO CRY. AND I'LL ALWAYS REMEMBER THAT NIGHT AS A PERFECT NIGHT. A PERFECT NIGHT WHEN I SAW HER HAPPY.

LAST DAY

BY LYNDA BARRY © 1989

TODAY WAS OUR LAST DAY OF SCHOOL. IN LANGUAGE ARTS MISS EVANGELINE ASKED US TO WRITE OUR FEELINGS ON THIS YEAR, INCLUDING BAD, GOOD, BEAUTIFUL, MESSED-UP. THE TITLE OF MINE WAS <u>MY SUCKIEST YEAR</u>

THIS IS A RIP OFF, MAN. I THOUGHT WE WERE SUPPOSED TO HAVE A PARTY

ALL THE OTHER CLASSES GET PARTIES.

I KNOW

ARE WE GETTING GRADED ON THIS OR IS IT CREATIVE?

I ABOUT STARTED CRYING WHEN I WAS WRITING IT FROM REALIZING ALL MY PROBLEMS. HOW ME AND BRENDA WERE BEST FRIENDS SINCE THIRD GRADE UNTIL THIS YEAR AND NOW WHEN WE PASS IN THE HALL WE DON'T EVEN LOOK AT EACH OTHER. HOW BRIAN BANO USED ME AT CROFTON PARK. HOW I GOT RESTRICTION FROM MY MOM 900 TIMES.

I HATE THIS.

THIS ASSIGNMENT IS NO FAIR.

HEY. HOW DO YOU SPELL "PROCOL HARUM"?

DOES IT GOT AN "E"?

AND THEN THAT SONG? "THE WORLD IS A GHETTO"? IT'S TOTALLY TRUE. WARS, VIOLENCE, PREJUDICE AND ~~POLU~~ POLLUTION. NO PROBLEMS ENDED THIS YEAR. WHEN I TRY TO THINK OF THE BEAUTIFUL THINGS THAT HAPPENED? ALL I CAN THINK OF IS: MY MOM LET ME GET MY EARS PIERCED. THAT, AND MY NEW PURPLE PANTS FROM THE CUBE.

FORGET IT. I'M NOT DOING IT. THERE'S NO WAY IT CAN AFFECT MY GRADE.

WE'RE SUPPOSED TO HAVE A PARTY ON THE LAST DAY, MAN.

YOU GOIN' TO CINDY'S THING TONIGHT?

HEY.

AT THE END OF THE PAPER MISS EVANGELINE SAID TO WRITE DOWN A WISH FOR OUR FUTURE, THEN TOLD US TO HITCH OUR WAGONS TO A STAR. I GOT STUCK ON: SHOULD I MAKE A WISH FOR THE EARTH, LIKE PEACE? OR A WISH FOR ME, FOR MY LIFE? AND BEFORE I COULD WRITE IT THE BELL RANG AND MISS EVANGELINE SAID DON'T PASS YOUR PAPERS IN, KEEP THEM. KEEP THEM, BECAUSE WHEN YOU ARE OLDER YOU WILL WANT TO REMEMBER.

FINALLY

RIIIINNN.G...

AW-RITE!

RING!!

61

VACATION DAY

BY LYNDA BARRY ⊙⊙⊙⊙⊙⊙ ⊙ ⊙ ⊙ 1989

"ARE YOU READY?" MY MOM SHOUTS UP THE STAIRS. "UNCLE JOHN WILL BE HERE ANY SECOND." A HORN HONKS OUTSIDE AND I CAN HEAR THE BIG CAR ENGINE STOP. "GOD DAMN HIM" MY MOTHER SAYS. "HE'LL WAKE UP THE WHOLE NEIGHBORHOOD." IT'S 6 AM. I CAN HEAR THE BIRDS SINGING.

MY SISTER MARLYS DRAGS A SUITCASE PAST MY BEDROOM DOOR. "YOU'RE MAKING US LATE" SHE SAYS TO ME. THEN SHE DRAGS IT TO THE STAIRS AND I HEAR HER SAY "UH-OH" THEN THE SOUND OF IT CRASHING DOWN THE STAIRWAY AND MY MOTHER SHOUTING "FOR THE LOVE OF GOD!" THE HORN HONKS AGAIN. UNCLE JOHN IS TAKING US TO OUR VACATION AT OUR GRANDMA MULLEN'S.

62

MY MOM SHOUTS "JESUS! MARLYS, RUN OUT THERE AND TELL HIM IF HE HONKS THAT HORN ONE MORE TIME I'LL WRING HIS NECK!" THEN THE FRONT DOOR OPENS AND SLAMS SHUT AND I HEAR MARLYS SCREAMING "MY MOM SAYS KNOCK IT OFF!" I TAKE MY SUITCASE AND GO DOWNSTAIRS. "BYE, MOM" I SAY. "BE GOOD." SHE SAYS BACK. "WATCH YOUR SISTER." "OK" I SAY. MY UNCLE HONKS THE HORN. "HE'S TRYING TO KILL ME" MOM SAYS.

I HAVE TO ADMIT, UNCLE JOHN IS MY FAVOR-ITE UNCLE, EVEN THOUGH MY MOM DOES HATE HIM FOR BEING MY DAD'S BROTHER. "MAVIS! MAVIS!" I HEAR HIM YELLING. THAT'S MY MOTHER'S NAME. "MAVIS! COME OUT HERE AND SAY HELLO."
  "YOU TELL HIM TO GO TO HELL." MY MOM SAYS. "OK" I SAY AND I OPEN THE DOOR AND SEE MARLYS IN THE FRONT SEAT LAUGHING AND SHOVING FRITOS IN HER MOUTH, AND OUR WHOLE STREET LOOKING LIKE IT'S ON BEAUTIFUL FIRE.

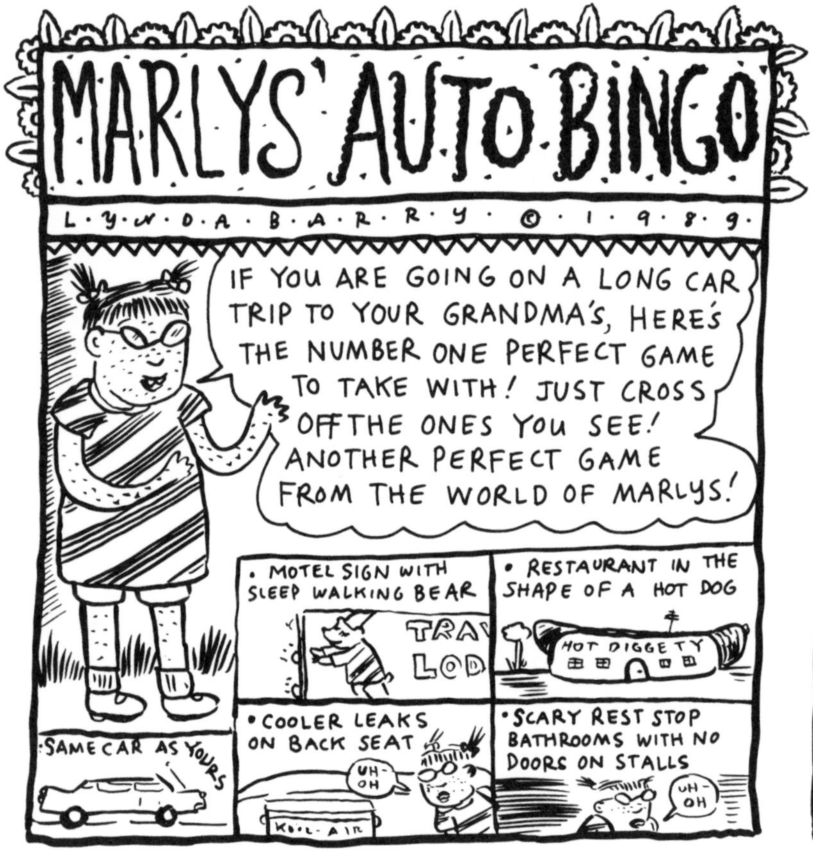
MARLYS' AUTO BINGO
LYNDA BARRY © 1989
IF YOU ARE GOING ON A LONG CAR TRIP TO YOUR GRANDMA'S, HERE'S THE NUMBER ONE PERFECT GAME TO TAKE WITH! JUST CROSS OFF THE ONES YOU SEE! ANOTHER PERFECT GAME FROM THE WORLD OF MARLYS!
• MOTEL SIGN WITH SLEEP WALKING BEAR
TRAV
LOD
• RESTAURANT IN THE SHAPE OF A HOT DOG
HOT DIGGETY
• SAME CAR AS YOURS
• COOLER LEAKS ON BACK SEAT
UH-OH
KOOL-AIR
• SCARY REST STOP BATHROOMS WITH NO DOORS ON STALLS
UH-OH

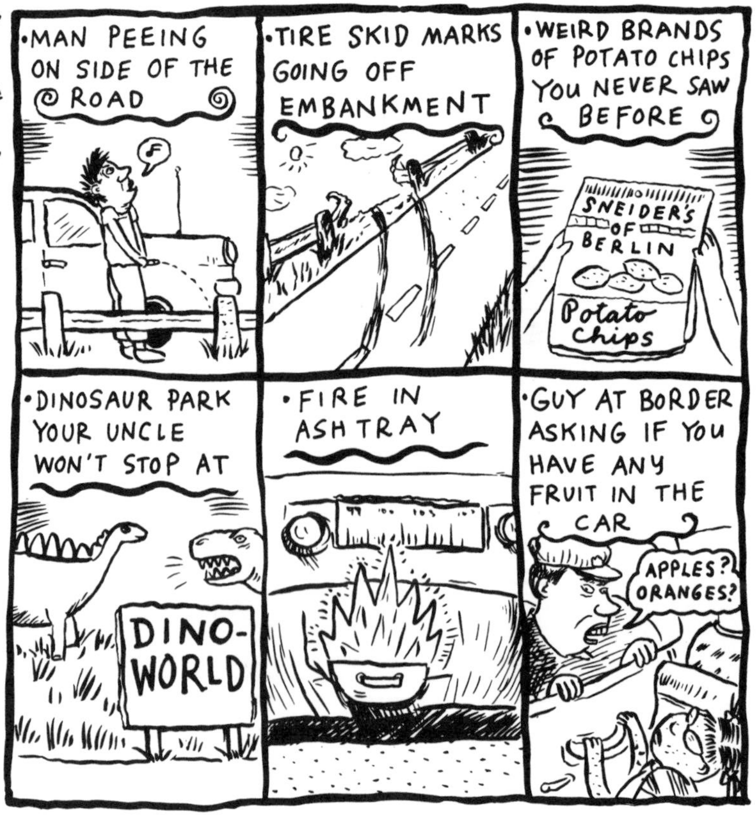
• MAN PEEING ON SIDE OF THE ROAD
F
• TIRE SKID MARKS GOING OFF EMBANKMENT
• WEIRD BRANDS OF POTATO CHIPS YOU NEVER SAW BEFORE
SNEIDER'S OF BERLIN
Potato Chips
• DINOSAUR PARK YOUR UNCLE WON'T STOP AT
DINO-WORLD
• FIRE IN ASHTRAY
• GUY AT BORDER ASKING IF YOU HAVE ANY FRUIT IN THE CAR
APPLES? ORANGES?

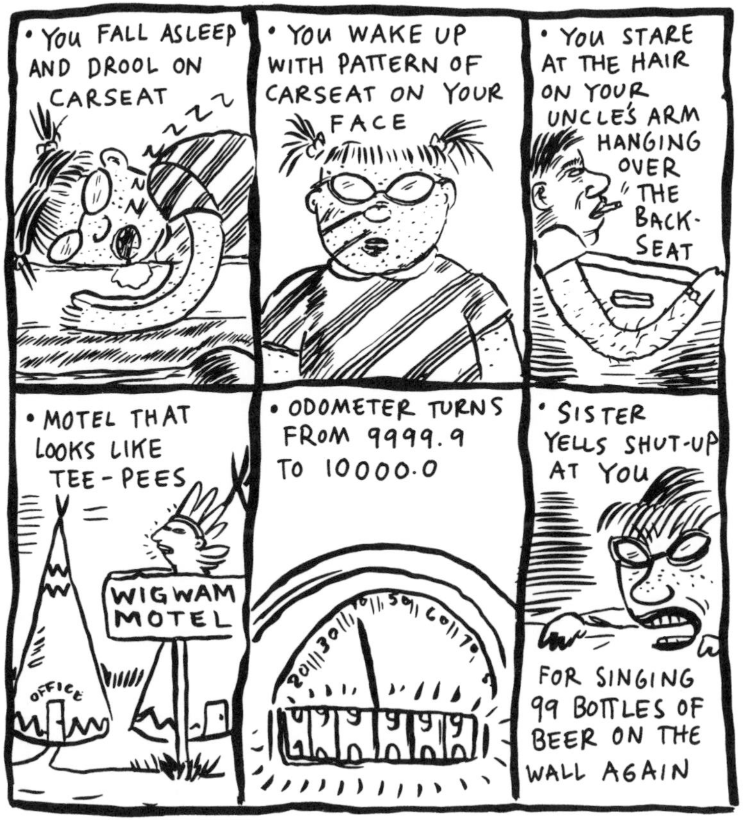
• YOU FALL ASLEEP AND DROOL ON CARSEAT
Z Z Z
• YOU WAKE UP WITH PATTERN OF CARSEAT ON YOUR FACE
• YOU STARE AT THE HAIR ON YOUR UNCLE'S ARM HANGING OVER THE BACK-SEAT
• MOTEL THAT LOOKS LIKE TEE-PEES
WIGWAM MOTEL
OFFICE
• ODOMETER TURNS FROM 9999.9 TO 10000.0
• SISTER YELLS SHUT-UP AT YOU
FOR SINGING 99 BOTTLES OF BEER ON THE WALL AGAIN

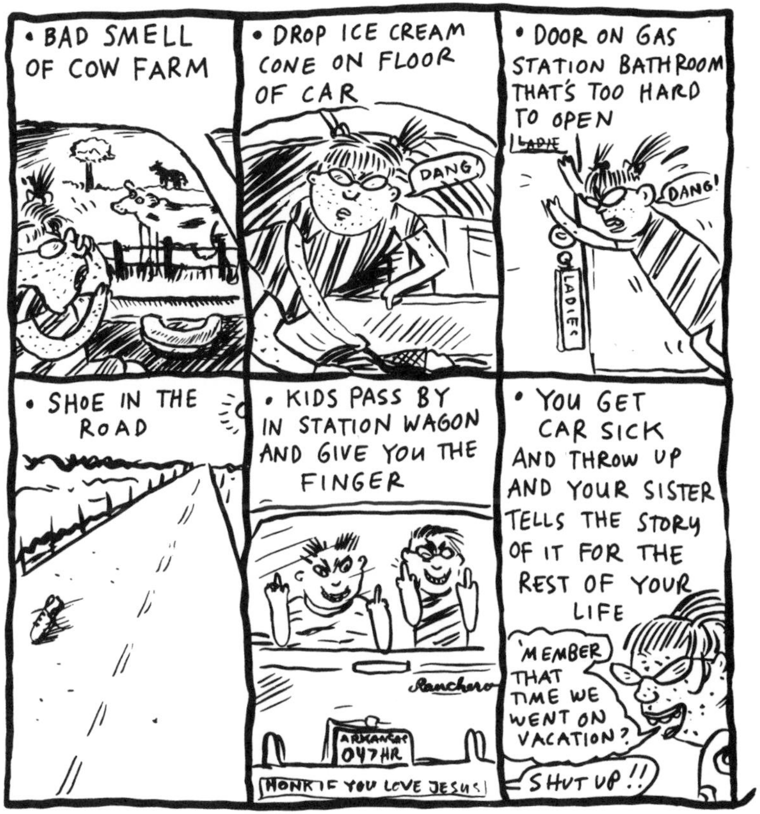
• BAD SMELL OF COW FARM
• DROP ICE CREAM CONE ON FLOOR OF CAR
DANG!
• DOOR ON GAS STATION BATHROOM THAT'S TOO HARD TO OPEN
DANG!
LADIES
• SHOE IN THE ROAD
• KIDS PASS BY IN STATION WAGON AND GIVE YOU THE FINGER
Ranchero
HONK IF YOU LOVE JESUS!
• YOU GET CAR SICK AND THROW UP AND YOUR SISTER TELLS THE STORY OF IT FOR THE REST OF YOUR LIFE
'MEMBER THAT TIME WE WENT ON VACATION?
SHUT UP!!

THE·LAST·MILES

BY LYNDA BARRY © 1989

IT WAS THE HOT MIDDLE OF THE NIGHT, PITCH BLACK ON THE HIGHWAY WITH ALL THE WINDOWS ROLLED DOWN. MY UNCLE WAS DRIVING AND MY SISTER MARLYS WAS KONKED OUT IN THE BACK SEAT.

FOR THE LOVE OF CHRIST, IT'S HOT.

YEAH. WE'RE GETTING CLOSE NOW.

WE WERE DRIVING STRAIGHT THROUGH TO SAVE MONEY ON MOTELS. DRIVING TO MY GRANDMA MULLEN'S. "I HOPE TO GOD THAT AIR CONDITIONER'S WORKING WHEN WE GET THERE" MY UNCLE SAID. I COUNTED. WE LEFT OUR HOUSE 18 HOURS AGO.

UP IN THE SKY THERE WERE A MILLION STARS AND IN OUR HEAD LIGHTS, BUGS FLEW UP. THE RADIO WAS PLAYING A SONG WITH A TRAIN IN IT, A MAN LISTENING TO THE TRAIN AND THEN HIM WONDERING WHERE SOMEONE WENT, AND I HAD A FEELING OF FLOATING. STARING OUT THE WINDOW AND JUST FLOATING.

AND THEN I MUST HAVE FALLEN ASLEEP BECAUSE THE NEXT THING I HEARD WAS THE SOUND OF A PACKAGE OF DOUGHNUTS HITTING THE SEAT, MY UNCLE TOSSING THEM THROUGH THE WINDOW IN THE BRIGHT SUN, STANDING OUTSIDE THE GROCERY STORE LAUGHING WITH COFFEE IN HIS HAND. "TEN MILES TO GO" HE SAID. "IT WAS A SON OF A BITCH, BUT WE DID IT."

67

TAKING SIDES

BY LYNDA BARRY © 1989

"THIS AIN'T NO VACATION" MY SISTER SAYS TO ME AS SOON AS MY GRANDMA MULLEN LEAVES THE ROOM. "STUCK AT THIS STUPID PLACE. I HATE THIS STUPID PLACE." "SHUT-UP" I TELL HER AND I PRAY MY GRANDMA WON'T HEAR.

THIS IS THE HOUSE DAD GREW UP IN.

SO?

DON'T MEAN NOTHIN' TO ME.

I WANNA GO HOME.

"THERE'S NOTHING TO DO HERE! WHAT ARE WE EVEN SUPPOSED TO DO HERE?" MARLYS SAYS, AND THEN MY GRANDMA COMES IN WITH A PLATE OF COOKIES, TELLING US THAT THEY'RE SNICKERDOODLES AND HOW OUR DAD USED TO LOVE THEM. "I DON'T WANT NONE." MARLYS SAYS, AND THEN ASKS FOR A PENCIL SO SHE CAN WRITE A LETTER TO MOM.

WELL, I'M NOT GOING TO FORCE YOU, DEAR.

HERE YOU GO, MAYBONNE

THANKS GRANDMA.

68

MY GRANDMA ASKS ME IF I CAN REMEMBER HOW I USED TO PLAY UNDER THE KITCHEN TABLE WHEN WE LIVED HERE WHEN I WAS 4. I DON'T REMEMBER IT, BUT I SAY YES. THEN SHE TRIES TO SAY SOME WORDS ABOUT THE DIVORCE AND SHE KNOWS IT'S BEEN HARD FOR US. THEN SHE ASKS US HOW IS OUR MOM, AND MARLYS SAYS "PERFECT."

WELL, YOU BE SURE TO WRITE IN YOUR LETTER THAT SHE'S IN OUR PRAYERS. YOU TELL YOUR MOM WE'RE THINKING ABOUT HER.

THAT NIGHT I WAKE UP FROM SOME TALKING DOWNSTAIRS. A MAN'S VOICE THAT I SWEAR TO GOD IS MY DAD'S. "NO RAY." MY GRANDMA SAYS. RAY. HIS <u>NAME</u>! "THEY'RE NOT READY YET." SHE TELLS HIM WE'RE ASLEEP, NOT TO BOTHER US, THAT SHE NEEDS TO TALK TO US, ESPECIALLY MARLYS, AND I HEAR FEET ON THE STAIRS AND AS THE DOOR OPENS I CLOSE MY EYES TIGHT AND LAY PERFECTLY STILL.

69

HI, DAD

BY L Y N D A xx B A R R Y ©89

WHEN I WOKE UP I COULDN'T REMEMBER WHERE I WAS. I COULD HEAR A CAKE MIXER GOING DOWNSTAIRS AND MY SISTER MARLYS TALKING LOUD. THEN I WENT "OH. I'M AT MY GRANDMA'S. I'M ON VACATION." OUTSIDE ON A TREE WAS A HALF RED BIRD LIKE I NEVER SAW BEFORE. THEN I REMEMBERED LAST NIGHT.

I HEARD MY DAD DOWNSTAIRS TALKING AND I KNEW IT WASN'T A DREAM I HAD. HE WAS REALLY HERE. THE FIRST THING I THOUGHT WAS HOW MOM WAS GOING TO KILL US. SHE DIDN'T WANT US EVER SEEING HIM AGAIN. EVER. IF SHE KNEW HE WAS GOING TO BE HERE WE NEVER COULD HAVE COME. MY GOAL WAS: JUST ACT NORMAL.

70

WHEN I CAME INTO THE KITCHEN MY LIFE FELT LIKE A MOVIE WHERE THE PROJECTOR STOPS AND YOU STARE AT THE BIG PICTURE FROZEN AND TURNING BROWN IN THE MIDDLE, BURNING UP. HIM SITTING THERE, ME SAYING "HI DAD", MY GRANDMA SMILING TOO BIG AND THE SOUND OF MY SISTER WITH A CRAZY LOOK ON HER FACE YELLING "SURPRISE!" EVERYTHING STARTING TO SPIN.

THEN THE PICTURE TURNS NORMAL, ONLY NOW, I'M THE AUDIENCE WATCHING ME. I WATCH ME PRETEND TO ACT EXCITED. I WATCH ME EAT THE SCRAMBLED EGGS AND I HEAR MY VOICE TELLING HIM LIES ABOUT SCHOOL, ABOUT MY LIFE. EVERYTHING LOOKING SO FAR AWAY, WATCHING UNTIL THE PICTURE TURNS BLACK.

71

WATCH ME

BY LYNDA BARRY © 1989 xxxx

MY SISTER LOVES IT THAT OUR DAD IS BACK. I LIKE IT OK, BUT TO ME IT'S STILL IN A WAY A FREAK OUT. PLUS, HOW LONG IS HE BACK FOR? I CAN'T ASK HIM THAT QUESTION.

DAD! DAD! WATCH!

♪LA KOOKA RATCHA! LA KOOKA RATCHA!♪

DAD! WATCH ME!

I CAN'T DO IT IF YOU DON'T WATCH!

DAD!

LAST NIGHT HE TOOK MARLYS TO CATCH NIGHTCRAWLERS FOR FISHING. THEY WENT IN THE GARDEN WITH A FLASHLIGHT AND A COFFEE CAN FULL OF DIRT. ME AND GRANDMA STAYED IN THE KITCHEN DOING THE DISHES AND SHE TOLD ME I WAS OLD ENOUGH TO KNOW HOW MY DAD QUIT DRINKING THROUGH JESUS CHRIST. ALSO THAT HIS NERVES WERE SHOT TO HELL.

YOU KIDS GO EASY ON HIM, YOU UNDERSTAND?

HE'S HAD IT ROUGH.

SHE TOLD ME IT WAS MR. LUDERMYER FROM NEXT DOOR WHO HELPED HIM SEE THE LIGHT AND ALSO GAVE HIM A JOB AT LUDERMYER MEATS. THEN THE SCREEN DOOR SLAMMED, MARLYS RUNNING IN WITH THE COFFEE CAN YELLING "WE GOT 20!" THROUGH THE WINDOW I COULD SEE MY DAD LIGHTING A CIGARETTE AND THEN LEANING AGAINST THE CLOTHESLINE POLE. "GO OUT THERE AND TELL HIM YOU'RE PROUD OF HIM" MY GRANDMA SAID.

THE GRASS WAS WET UNDER MY FEET AS I CROSSED THE BACK YARD AND WHEN MY DAD SAW ME, HE TURNED ON THE FLASHLIGHT AND MADE A LIT UP CIRCLE FOR ME TO WALK IN. I COULD HEAR A DOG START BARKING FAR AWAY AND MY DAD SAYING SOMETHING ABOUT MOSQUITOS AND THEN ME JUST STANDING THERE AND STANDING THERE, FEELING MY GRANDMOTHER WATCHING FROM THE WINDOW.

73

FISHING with MARLYS

L Y N D A ✳ BIG 'UN ✳ BARRY © 1989

OK. WHO EVER DOESN'T KNOW FISHING CAN LEARN IT FROM ME. FIRST CATCH A SLUG OF WORMS AND PUT THEM IN A COFFEE CAN WITH HALF WET DIRT.

WARNING ABOUT WORMS!!

IF YOU GET THE DIRT _TOO WET_ THE WORM WILL BE A GROSS _OUT_! IT WILL DIE AND SWELL UP!

IF THE DIRT IS TOO DRY, THE WORM WILL BE _CRUNCHY_! DEAD + SHRIVELED!

SOGGED OUT

LIKE BACON

THEN GO WITH YOUR DAD, YOUR UNCLE JOHN, YOU, AND YOUR STUPID SISTER WHO KEEPS ACTING LIKE TODAY IS THE WORST DAY OF HER LIFE, TO THE RIVER PAST THE A+W. HOLD YOUR DAD'S HAND. BE IN CHARGE OF THE WORMS.

EXCUSE ME. CAN I ASK YOU A CERTAIN QUESTION?

SHUT UP.

ARE YOU IN REALITY AN IDIOT?

SHUT UP!

HEY YOU TWO. NO FIGHTS!

MAXWELL HOUSE

LET YOUR DAD DO THE BAIT PART AND THROW IT IN THE WATER. THEN KEEP YOUR EYES PEELED ON THAT BOBBER THING, FOR IF IT GOES DOWN. THAT EQUALS A FISH BITE! THEN YANK IT UP AND SWING IT BY YOUR DAD SO YOU DON'T HAVE TO SEE HOW THE HOOK WENT UP THE FISH LIPS. AFTER, WHEN THE FISH IS IN THE YELLOW BUCKET, YOU CAN PET HIM.

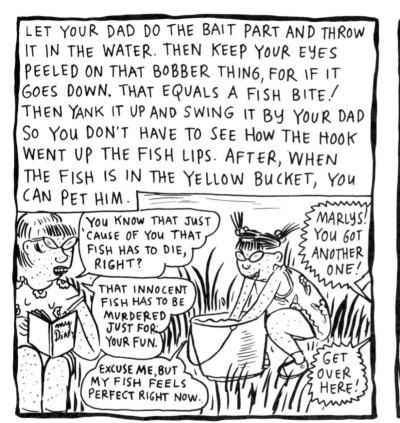

AND EVEN IF YOUR SISTER TRIES TO MAKE YOU FEEL ROTTEN BY WRITING IN HER DIARY SOME VEGETARIAN TRAGEDY POEMS ABOUT YOU BEING A FISH KILLER, IGNORE HER BECAUSE RIGHT BEFORE YOU'RE SUP- POSED TO GO BACK, YOU CAN SUDDENLY TRANSFORM TO A FISH SAVIOR BY TIPPING THE YELLOW BUCKET BACK INTO THE RIVER.

75

HIGH·DIVE·

Lynda Barry © 1989

IT'S AGAINST THE LAW TO MARRY YOUR OWN
COUSIN AND IT'S PERVERTED AND NOT THAT
I WOULD EVER WANT TO ANYWAY. ALL THAT
I'M TRYING TO SAY IS, HOW COME ROYLTON
JAMES HAS TO BE MY COUSIN? WHY CAN'T
HE BE SOME ONE ELSES, SO I WON'T HAVE
TO FEEL SO WEIRD ABOUT HOW I FEEL?

MY MOM SAID
I'M SUPPOSED
TO TAKE YOU GUYS TO
THE POOL WITH
ME. YA COMIN'?

BEAUTIFUL
EYES WITH
LONG
EYE
LASHES →

LONG
HAIR
↓

GORGEOUS
LIPS →

NOT THAT I WOULD EVEN GET A CHANCE
WITH HIM IN REAL LIFE. IF HE WASN'T
MY COUSIN, IN REAL LIFE I PROBABLY
WOULDN'T EVEN KNOW HIM. HE DOES PER-
FECT DIVES. WHEN I WATCH HIM STANDING
ON THE DIVING BOARD WITH HIS ARMS OUT,
I FEEL LIKE I COULD THROW UP OR FAINT
FROM HIS PERFECTION.

YOU GOT A CRUSH ON ROYLTON.

AS IF. DON'T EITHER.
HE'S OUR COUSIN IF
YOU DON'T REMEMBER

ITS
TRUE LOVE
FOR YOU
BUT NOT
FOR HIM.

YOU GOT
A CRUSH
ON HIM.

YOU
DO.

SHUT UP AND
FLAKE OFF →

HE LAYS ON THE TOWEL NEXT TO ME AND SAYS HOW MUCH HE HATES HIS MOM AND HIS DAD AND HOW HE'S GOING TO LEARN GUITAR AND HOW HE KNOWS PEOPLE WHO GET HIGH, AND I STARE AT THE DROPS OF WATER ON HIS BACK AND THE LIGHT ON HIS WET HAIR MAKING COLORED SHINES, THE TAG ON THE BACK OF HIS TRUNKS STICKING OUT, THE SCAR ON HIS LEG.

UM... HOW DID YOU GET THAT SCAR, ROYLTON?

♪ UM... HOW ♪ DIDJA GET THAT SCAR, ROYLTON?

THEN HE SUDDENLY STOPS TALKING AND WATCHES A GIRL CLIMBING OUT OF THE POOL. HE SAYS WHAT DO I THINK OF HER. SHES TAN AND DEVELOPED. "SHE LOOKS LIKE A SNOB" I SAY. "WHO IS SHE?" "NO-BODY." HE SAYS, THEN JUST MICROSCOPES HIS EYES ON HER AS SHE CLIMBS THE HIGH DIVE, RUNS, BOUNCES HIGH AND JACK KNIFES, TOES POINTED. IT'S A GOOD THING ROYLTON IS MY COUSIN. I'D NEVER BE ABLE TO DIVE LIKE THAT IN A MILLION YEARS.

WOW!

MAN! SHE'S LIKE IN A MOVIE! THAT'S EXACTLY WHAT I'M GONNA LOOK LIKE! JUST LIKE THAT GIRL.

BOY SHE SURE PICKED AN UGLY BATHING SUIT.

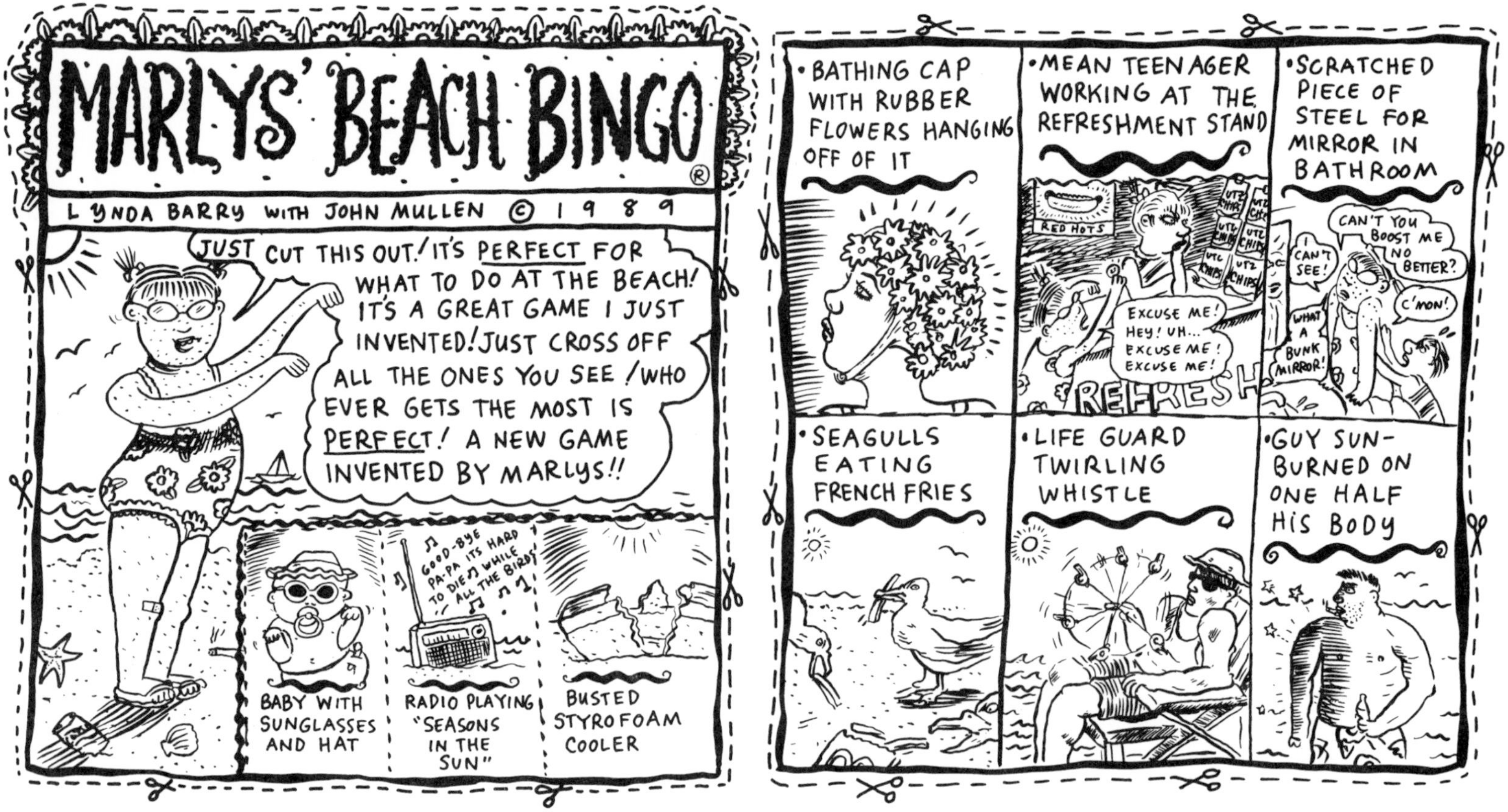
MARLYS' BEACH BINGO®
LYNDA BARRY WITH JOHN MULLEN © 1989
JUST CUT THIS OUT! IT'S PERFECT FOR WHAT TO DO AT THE BEACH! IT'S A GREAT GAME I JUST INVENTED! JUST CROSS OFF ALL THE ONES YOU SEE! WHO EVER GETS THE MOST IS PERFECT! A NEW GAME INVENTED BY MARLYS!!
BABY WITH SUNGLASSES AND HAT
GOOD-BYE PA-PA ITS HARD TO DIE WHILE ALL THE BIRDS
RADIO PLAYING "SEASONS IN THE SUN"
BUSTED STYROFOAM COOLER
•BATHING CAP WITH RUBBER FLOWERS HANGING OFF OF IT
•MEAN TEEN AGER WORKING AT THE REFRESHMENT STAND
RED HOTS
UTZ CHIPS
EXCUSE ME! HEY! UH... EXCUSE ME! EXCUSE ME!
REFRESH
•SCRATCHED PIECE OF STEEL FOR MIRROR IN BATHROOM
I CAN'T SEE!
CAN'T YOU BOOST ME NO BETTER?
C'MON!
WHAT A BUNK MIRROR!
•SEAGULLS EATING FRENCH FRIES
•LIFE GUARD TWIRLING WHISTLE
•GUY SUN-BURNED ON ONE HALF HIS BODY

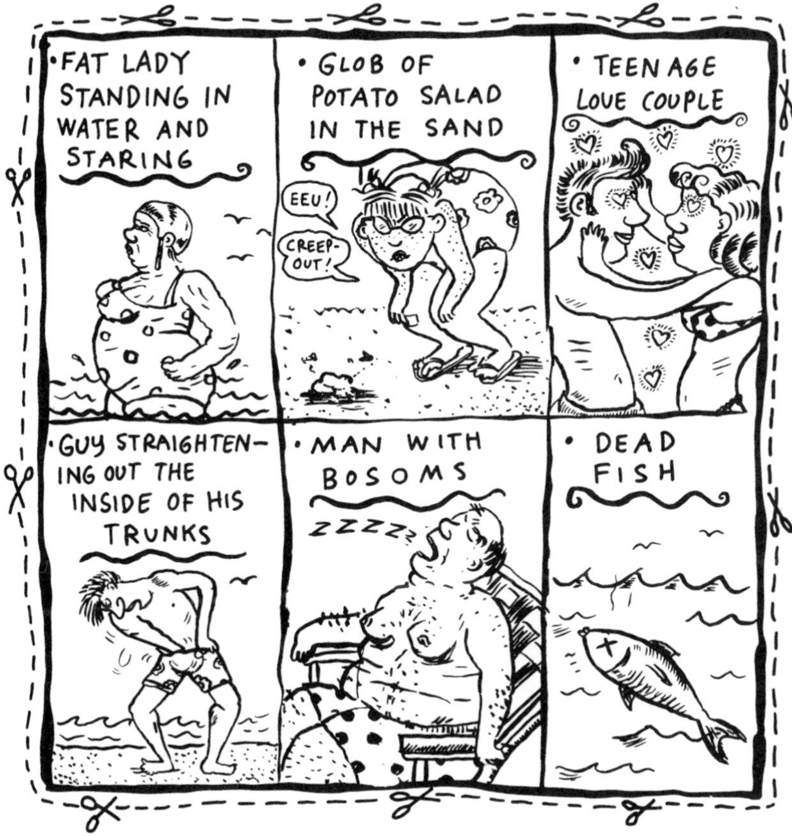

•FAT LADY STANDING IN WATER AND STARING
•GLOB OF POTATO SALAD IN THE SAND
EEU!
CREEP-OUT!
•TEENAGE LOVE COUPLE
•GUY STRAIGHTENING OUT THE INSIDE OF HIS TRUNKS
•MAN WITH BOSOMS
ZZZZZ
•DEAD FISH

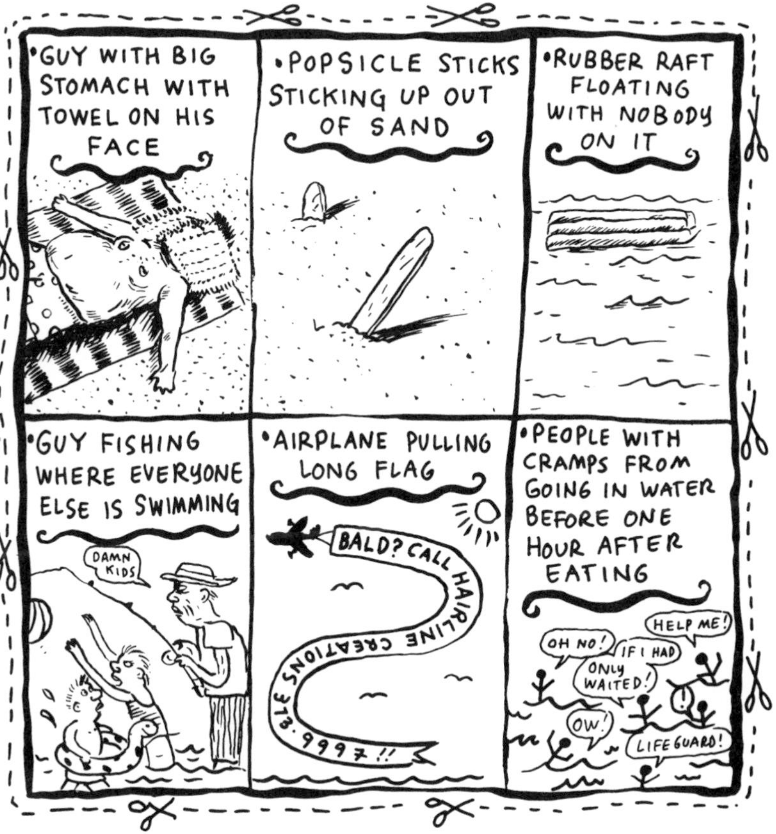

•GUY WITH BIG STOMACH WITH TOWEL ON HIS FACE
•POPSICLE STICKS STICKING UP OUT OF SAND
•RUBBER RAFT FLOATING WITH NOBODY ON IT
•GUY FISHING WHERE EVERYONE ELSE IS SWIMMING
DAMN KIDS
•AIRPLANE PULLING LONG FLAG
BALD? CALL HAIRLINE CREATIONS ELE·9997!!
•PEOPLE WITH CRAMPS FROM GOING IN WATER BEFORE ONE HOUR AFTER EATING
OH NO!
HELP ME!
IF I HAD ONLY WAITED!
OW!
LIFEGUARD!

THE LAST BLOCKS

· L · Y · N · D · A ❋ B · A · R · R · Y ❋ © ❋ 1 9 8 9 ❋

WE HAD SPENT THE WHOLE DAY AT THE BEACH, THEN ON THE WAY HOME, OUR COUSIN ROYLTON JAMES SAID DID WE WANT TO GO TO THE A+W AND HOW MUCH MONEY DID WE HAVE COMBINED. IT EQUALLED $5.49. ENOUGH FOR A LOT.

NO WAY!

THATS MY $5.00 BIRTHDAY MONEY!

YOU GUYS ONLY ADDED IN 49¢!

GIVE IT BACK!

FORGET IT!

C'MON MARLYS

YEAH, MARLYS

PLEEEESE?

WE SAT AT THE PICNIC TABLE BY THE PARKING LOT WAITING FOR THEM TO CALL OUR ORDER. MARLYS TOLD US HER BODY KEPT FEELING LIKE IT WAS STILL UNDER WATER. I SHOWED ROYLTON MY SUNBURN MARKS AND HE SHOWED ME WHERE HE GOT STITCHES FROM HIS OPERATION WHEN HE WAS BORN. IT WAS RIGHT BY HIS BATHING SUIT LINE.

IT STILL FEELS LIKE THERE'S WAVES ON ME.

I HAD, LIKE, AN INVERTED HERNIA OR SOMETHING. MY GUTS WERE HANGING OUT.

LIKE WAVES ARE HITTING ME.

THAT BIRD OVER THERE JUST TOOK A CRAP. DID YOU GUYS SEE IT?

OH ROYLTON!

MAN, THATS WAY WORSE THAN MY SUNBURN! DID YOU SEE MY SUNBURN?

WHEN THEY CALLED OUR NUMBER I SUDDENLY GOT SO STARVED I THOUGHT I WAS GOING TO FAINT. THE FRENCH FRIES WERE THE MOST DELICIOUS ONES IN ALL THE WORLD. ROYLTON KEPT TRYING TO FREAK US OUT BY DUNKING HIS FRIES IN HIS MILK SHAKE AND EATING THEM. THEN HE SHOWED US THE CONTEST OF: WHO EVER HAS THE MOST PICKLES IN THEIR HAMBURGER IS THE COOLEST. HE GOT 2, I GOT 2, AND MARLYS GOT 6. THE WORLD'S RECORD.

HERE ROYLTON. HAVE IT.

NO, THATS OK. MARLYS.

NO. HAVE IT. I GOT 5 MORE. "PETTY CASH TO ME."

OK MAN. THANKS.

HEY MAN. WHAT ABOUT ME?

THE MANAGER YELLED OUT THE WINDOW TO QUIT FEEDING THE BIRDS AND QUIT BASKET-BALLING THE WRAPPERS INTO THE GARBAGE CAN AND THEN ROYLTON SAID WE BETTER GO OR WE WOULD BE LATE FOR DINNER. I REMEMBER FEELING SO TIRED THAT I COULD HARDLY WALK THE 13 BLOCKS TO MY GRANDMAS. THEN AROUND THE CORNER COMES MY DAD'S CAR. "HOP IN" HE SAID. I NEVER FELT ANYTHING AS GOOD AS SITTING IN THE BACK SEAT, RIDING THE LAST BLOCKS HOME WITH MY EYES CLOSED.

HAPPY BIRTHDAY

·B·Y· ·L·Y·N·D·A· ·B·A·R·R·Y· © 1·9·8·9

MY PERFECT BIRTHDAY. BY MARLYS. A STORY BY MARLYS. ONCE UPON A TIME IT WAS THE BIRTHDAY OF MARLYS. EVERYBODY ALWAYS KEPT SAYING I CANNOT WAIT FOR THIS DAY. SOME PEOPLE KEPT SAYING MARLYS IS CONCEITED. THEN THEY WERE SORRY BECAUSE THEY WERE NOT INVITED TO THE GREAT BIRTHDAY PARTY. LIKE FOR EXAMPLE HER SISTER.

WHAT ARE YOU DOING?

SHUT UP.

YOU OK?

SHUT UP.

ON HER SISTER'S BIRTHDAY MARLYS MADE A PERSONAL CAKE AND BLEW UP BALLOONS THE LONG KIND THAT YOU GET A HEADACHE DOING AND MARLYS MADE A CARD: TO THE BEST SISTER. THEN ON MARLYS'S BIRTHDAY MAYBONNE DIDN'T EVEN REMEMBER. MARLYS KEPT GOING IT IS MY BIRTHDAY BUT ALL MAYBONNE SAID IS "I KNOW." BUT THAT DIDN'T MATTER TO MARLYS ONE BIT. MARLYS DIDN'T EVEN CARE. ON MARLYS'S BIRTHDAY THERE WAS A GIANT PARADE.

GRANDMA SAYS TO COME DOWNSTAIRS

IT'S MY BIRTHDAY.

I KNOW. WE GOTTA CLEAN THE GARAGE.

COME ON.

ON MARLYS'S BIRTHDAY EVERYBODY DID THE PEACE SIGN TO HER FROM CARS. SHE DESERVED IT. AT THE DRIVE IN THEY SAID PLEASE HAVE MORE FREE FRENCH FRIES. THEN MARLYS DROPPED A FRENCH FRY ON THE GROUND AND HER SISTER SCROUNGED IT AND ATE IT. THIS PROVES HER SISTER IS A SCROUNGE. MARLYS WAS NICE TO HER SISTER BUT HER SISTER THINKS SHE'S BIG. NOW IT'S TOO LATE AND I DON'T EVEN CARE. I'M STARTING TO LAUGH IT SERVES YOU RIGHT FOR HOW MEAN YOU ARE TO ME MAYBONNE I HATE YOU SO MUCH.

MARLYS!!

WHAT?!!

YOU GET DOWN HERE!

SHUT UP!

COMING!

I SAVED UP FIVE ALLOWENCES TO BUY YOU THAT LOVES FRESH LEMON SOAP AND OH DE LONDON PERFUME AND THEN IT'S MY BIRTHDAY AND YOU DIDN'T GIVE ME NOTHING. YOU OR GRANDMA. AND MOM DIDN'T CALL AND DAD DIDN'T CALL I HATE YOU ALL. YOU JUST WAIT. I'M GOING TO BE A MOVIE STAR. YOU WILL BE SO SORRY YOU TREATED ME LIKE THIS WHEN I GO ON A MOVIE AND TALK ABOUT HOW BAD YOU WERE. I WILL GO ON A MOVIE AND I WILL TELL THE WHOLE AUDIENCE HOW—

SA-PRIZE!

83

BACK to SCHOOL

BY LYNDA BARRY · ✿ ✿ ✿ ✿ ✿ © 1989

THIS YEAR WE'RE LIVING AT OUR GRANDMA'S. IT'S A LONG STORY WHY, BUT ONE THING IT MEANS IS A NEW SCHOOL. SELMER JR. HIGH FOR ME, AND MILFORD ELEMENTARY FOR MY SISTER. LAST NIGHT, I ALMOST WOKE UP MARLYS AND SAID "LET'S RUN AWAY."

THIS MORNING, CINDY LUDERMYER, THE SNOB OF THE WORLD FROM NEXT DOOR, RANG THE DOORBELL AND THEN STOOD IN THE DRIVEWAY WITH HER TWO SNOBBY FRIENDS DORIS BELL AND MARY HURLEY. MY GRAND-MA TOLD CINDY'S DAD TO TELL CINDY TO TAKE ME WITH HER ON THE FIRST DAY. AS IF I'M PITIFUL!

84

THEN ON THE WAY THERE, MARY HURLEY STARTS SMOKING AND CINDY AND DORIS TAKE DRAGS, THEN WHEN MARY SAYS TO ME "WANT A DRAG?", CINDY LUDERMYER SAYS "SHE DOESN'T SMOKE." AS IF SHE KNOWS MY LIFE! JUST BECAUSE MY DAD WORKS FOR HER DAD DOESN'T MEAN SHE CAN START CONTROLLING MY LIFE. I'M SICK OF PEOPLE CONTROLLING MY LIFE!

I TOLD CINDY EXCUSE ME, BUT YES I DO SO SMOKE, AND I TOOK A DRAG THEN MARY HURLEY SAYS "YOU CAN HAVE IT." IT WAS MYSTERIOUS! I DIDN'T KNOW, WAS IT BECAUSE I CONTAMINATED IT, OR WAS SHE BEING NICE? SHE SEEMS NICE BUT SHE COULD BE TWO FACED. SHE'S THE ONLY ONE WHO SAID BYE TO ME WHEN THE BELL RANG. DORIS AND CINDY JUST KEPT ON WALKING.

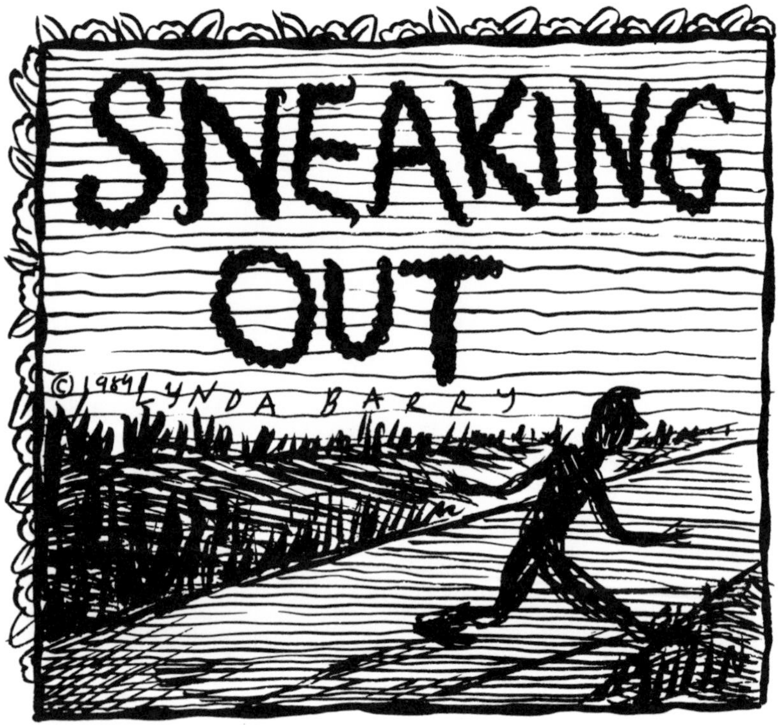
SNEAKING OUT
©1984 LYNDA BARRY

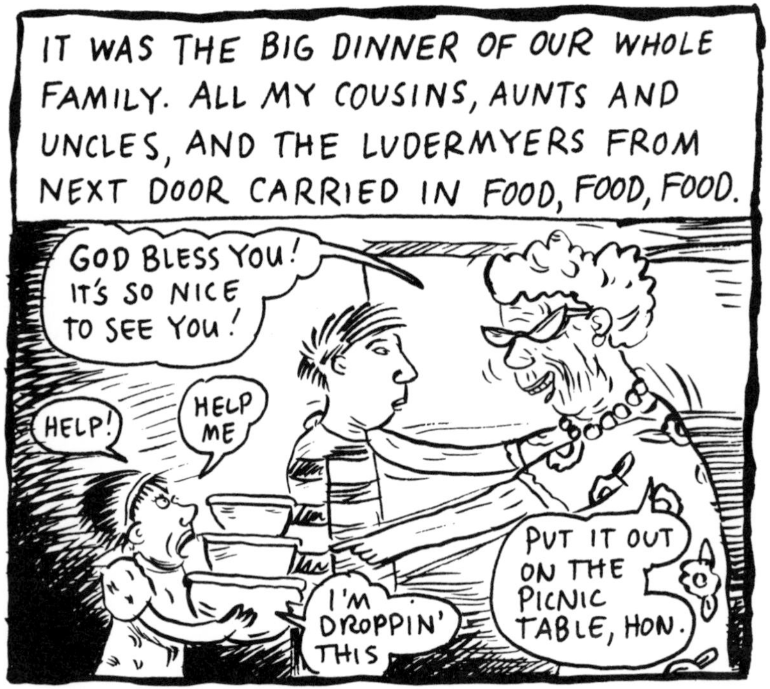
IT WAS THE BIG DINNER OF OUR WHOLE FAMILY. ALL MY COUSINS, AUNTS AND UNCLES, AND THE LUDERMYERS FROM NEXT DOOR CARRIED IN FOOD, FOOD, FOOD.
GOD BLESS YOU! IT'S SO NICE TO SEE YOU!
HELP!
HELP ME
I'M DROPPIN' THIS
PUT IT OUT ON THE PICNIC TABLE, HON.

TEN MILLION TONS OF FOOD WRAPPED IN ALCOA AND SARAN WRAP. THEN, BEFORE WE COULD EAT, MR. LUDERMYER MADE A TOAST TO MY DAD.

PRAISE GOD!

TO RAY. YOU HAD A LONG ROW TO HOE, BUT GOD DAMN IT, YOU HOED IT.

BEST GOD DAMN EMPLOYEE I GOT.

THE PARTY WAS FOR HIM QUITTING DRINKING. MY GRANDMA STARTED CRYING AND HUGGING MY DAD. SHE KEPT GIVING ME AND MY SISTER THE SIGNAL TO CRY AND HUG OUR DAD TOO.

HEY C'MON.

WHAT.

WE GOTTA GO STAND BY DAD.

HEY.

WHAT?

SHE KEPT GIVING OUR UNCLE JOHN THE SIGNAL TO TAKE THE PICTURES AND MY AUNT WILDA KEPT GIVING THE SIGNAL FOR EVERYONE ELSE TO QUIT STARING AND START EATING.

AFTER DINNER EVERYBODY SAT OUT IN THE BACKYARD LISTENING TO MOSTLY MR. LUDERMYER TALKING.

MY GRANDMA SAID DAD OWED HIS LIFE TO THAT MAN. MR. LUDERMYER WHO HELPED HIM OUT. MR. LUDERMYER WHO GAVE HIM THAT JOB.

I WATCHED HOW MR. LUDERMYER KEPT PUTTING HIS ARM AROUND MY DAD AND HOW MY DAD KEPT DRINKING MORE PEPSI, MORE PEPSI, MORE PEPSI.

THEN MY DAD STOOD UP AND PULLED OUT HIS CAR KEYS. "WHERE YOU GOING, RAY?" MY GRANDMA SAID. "CIGARETTES" MY DAD SAID.

"CHRIST, I MAY AS WELL COME WITH YOU" MR. LUDERMYER SAID. "BLOW THE DUST OFF OF ME." HE WAS GIVING MY GRANDMA A LOOK.

"NAW" SAID MY DAD. "I'LL BE RIGHT BACK" MY GRANDMA STOOD UP. "BRING THE KIDS WITH YOU, RAY." SHE SAID.

BUT HE WAS ALREADY DOWN THE DRIVEWAY. ALREADY DOWN THE DARK STREET.

TWO HOURS AFTER MY DAD STILL WASN'T BACK, MY AUNT WILDA STARTED SLAMMING THINGS AROUND IN THE KITCHEN.

WHERE'D HE GO FOR CIGARETTES, TIMBUKTU?

DOES HE THINK WE'RE IDIOTS?

I KNOW DAMN WELL WHERE HE IS.

WRAP!

"HE DOESN'T THINK OF ANYONE BUT HIMSELF" SHE SAID. "NEVER HAS AND NEVER WILL." SHE GOT HER BOWLS AND YELLED FOR HER KIDS TO GET THEIR COATS ON.

YOU SHUSH. YOU DON'T KNOW—

—OH DON'T I?

COME ON MOM. JESUS CHRIST.

EVERYONE WAS LEAVING. PRETTY SOON IT WAS JUST MY GRANDMA AND MR. LUDERMYER SITTING IN THE KITCHEN.

BELIEVE ME, NOLA. I KNOW EXACTLY HOW YOU FEEL.

GOT ANY MORE OF THAT CAKE HANDY?

I SAT ON THE BACK PORCH WITH MY LITTLE SISTER. SHE TOLD ME SHE WAS FEELING KIND OF SICK. I THOUGHT SHE WAS FAKING TO GET ATTENTION BUT THEN SHE THREW UP.

GRANDMA!

93

IN A WAY HER BARFING TURNED OUT TO BE A GOOD THING BECAUSE IT MADE MY GRANDMA COME RUNNING OUT AND IT TOOK HER MIND OFF MY DAD.

YES. YES. IT'S OK, HONEY. COME ON INSIDE.

YOU GONNA BE OK?

THE BAD PART ABOUT IT WAS IT MEANT I GOT STUCK WITH MR. LUDERMYER WHO STARTED TO GIVE ME HIS PHILOSOPHY ON LIFE.

LET A SMILE BE YOUR UMBRELLA.

THAT ABOUT SAYS IT ALL, DOESN'T IT?

HE STARTED SAYING HIS OBSERVATIONS ABOUT BEING A GOOD FATHER AND I ABOUT SAID IF YOU'RE SO PERFECT, HOW COME YOUR DAUGHTER IS ABOUT THE BIGGEST SLUT AT OUR SCHOOL?

AND I'VE HEARD MANY WORDS IN MY DAY BUT NONE AS BEAUTIFUL AS "I LOVE YOU DADDY"

AND RIGHT THEN CINDY LUDERMYER COMES OUT ON THEIR BACK PORCH AND SAYS "DAD. COME ON DAD. IT'S LATE." CINDY LUDERMYER AND ME HATE EACH OTHER.

DAD!

95

MR. LUDERMYER SAYS "IN A MINUTE, HONEY" AND THEN HE LOOKS AT ME LIKE THERE'S A MOVIE DOING A CLOSE UP OF HIS FACE ABOUT THE BEAUTY OF LIFE, AND ALL I CAN THINK IS: "YOU ARE SO STUPID."

THE TIME HAS COME...

FOR US TO PART

YEAH. GOODNIGHT.

THE ONLY REASON CINDY LUDERMYER WANTS HIM TO COME IN AND GO TO SLEEP IS BECAUSE SHE'S SNEAKING OUT TONIGHT.

EVERYONE IS. MY COUSIN ROYLTON JAMES SAID MEET AT THE ROPE SWING AT 2AM. BRING JUNGLE JUICE.

YOUR SISTER'S ASLEEP. DON'T YOU DARE WAKE HER.

OK. GOODNIGHT GRANDMA.

AND DON'T FORGET YOUR PRAYERS.

JUNGLE JUICE IS WHEN YOU KYPE INCHES OF EVERY KIND OF BOOZE AND MIX IT IN ONE JAR. THERE WASN'T ANY BOOZE IN MY GRANDMA'S HOUSE. AND I DIDN'T KNOW IF I EVEN FELT LIKE GOING ANYWAY.

WITH MY HYPERTENSION, I WON'T MAKE IT THROUGH THE NIGHT.

WE GOT TO FIND HIM.

NO. THE KIDS ARE SLEEPING. THEY'LL BE FINE.

97

I COULDN'T SLEEP. I KEPT WATCHING THE LIGHTED CLOCK GOING 11:00, MIDNIGHT, 1:00, 1:30 AND AT 20 TO 2 I ROLLED OFF THE BED QUIET SO I WOULDN'T WAKE UP MY SISTER.

OUTSIDE, THE GRASS SOAKED MY TENNIS SHOES BEFORE I GOT ACROSS THE FRONT YARD. THEN MR. LUDER-MYER'S STATION WAGON DROVE UP. I DUCKED IN THE BUSHES.

TURNS OUT CINDY LUDERMYER WAS IN THE BUSHES ALSO. "<u>DAMN</u>." SHE SAID. "<u>DAMN</u>." MR. LUDERMYER OPENED THE DOOR AND FOR A SECOND I THOUGHT IT WAS MY DAD WITH HIM.

IT WAS MY GRANDMA. "SHIP HIM OUT." MR. LUDERMYER SAID. "WHERE <u>IS</u> HE?" MY GRANDMA SAID. "HE HAS KIDS TO THINK ABOUT. HE HAS <u>ME</u> TO THINK ABOUT. HOW COULD HE DO THIS?"

I HATE TO SAY IT NOLA.

I KNOW. I KNOW.

WELL?

99

"IF THE S.O.B. CAN'T APPRECIATE ALL THE PEOPLE THAT BUSTED THEIR BUTTS FOR HIM, SHIP HIM OUT." MR. LUDERMYER LIT A CIGARETTE. "DON'T LET HIM THROUGH THAT DOOR."

I'D TELL HIM. I'D SAY RAY, I'VE HAD IT UP TO HERE.

YOU'RE ON YOUR OWN, MY GOOD MAN!

THEY WENT INTO MY GRANDMA'S HOUSE. CINDY LUDERMYER STOOD UP. "I'M SPLITTING." SHE SAID. "YOU COMING?" WE CUT ACROSS STREETS AND BACK YARDS AND CROSSED THE FOOTBRIDGE TO THE ROPE SWING.

MY COUSIN ROYLTON JAMES WAS STANDING SOAKING WET IN HIS UNDERWEAR DRINKING OUT OF A BOY SCOUT CANTEEN.
PATTY HERZOCK WAS HANGING OFF THE ROPE SWING IN HER BRA AND PANTIES

DAN AND RON GLYNN WERE THERE AND DORIS BELL AND MARY HURLEY. EVERYONE WAS IN THEIR UNDERWEAR. MY COUSIN YELLED "SKINNY DIP!" WHEN HE SAW US. PATTY HERZOCK DROPPED OFF THE ROPE SWING AND CAME UP SCREAMING.

"BYE" CINDY SAID TO ME AND RAN OVER TO DAN GLYNN AND JUMPED ON HIS BACK. A RADIO WAS PLAYING. A SONG ABOUT "IF HER DADDY'S RICH" AND DAN STARTED SINGING IT TO CINDY.

HEY HOG GIVE ME SOME!

THEN A GUY, TOM DONATO PUT HIS ARM AROUND ME AND GAVE ME SOME DRINKS OF HIS JUNGLE JUICE.

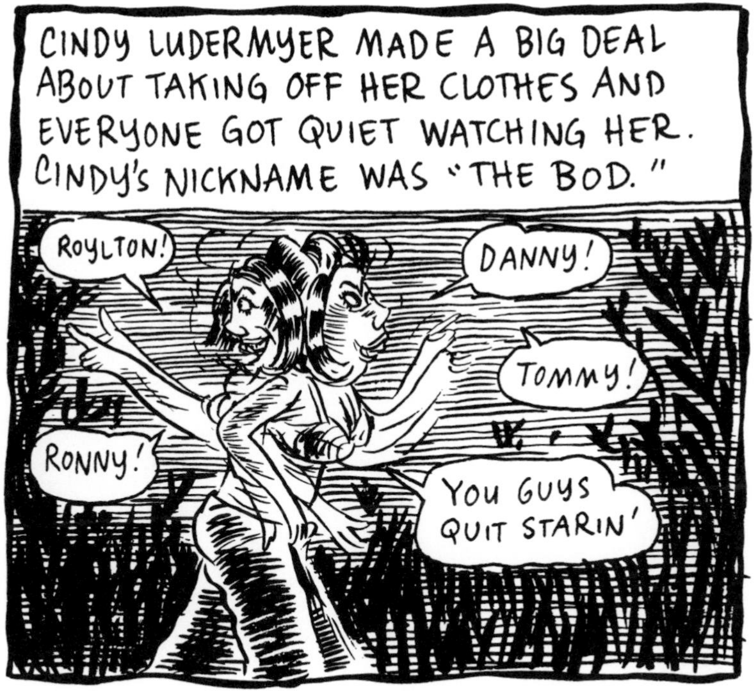
CINDY LUDERMYER MADE A BIG DEAL ABOUT TAKING OFF HER CLOTHES AND EVERYONE GOT QUIET WATCHING HER. CINDY'S NICKNAME WAS "THE BOD."
ROYLTON!
DANNY!
TOMMY!
RONNY!
YOU GUYS QUIT STARIN'

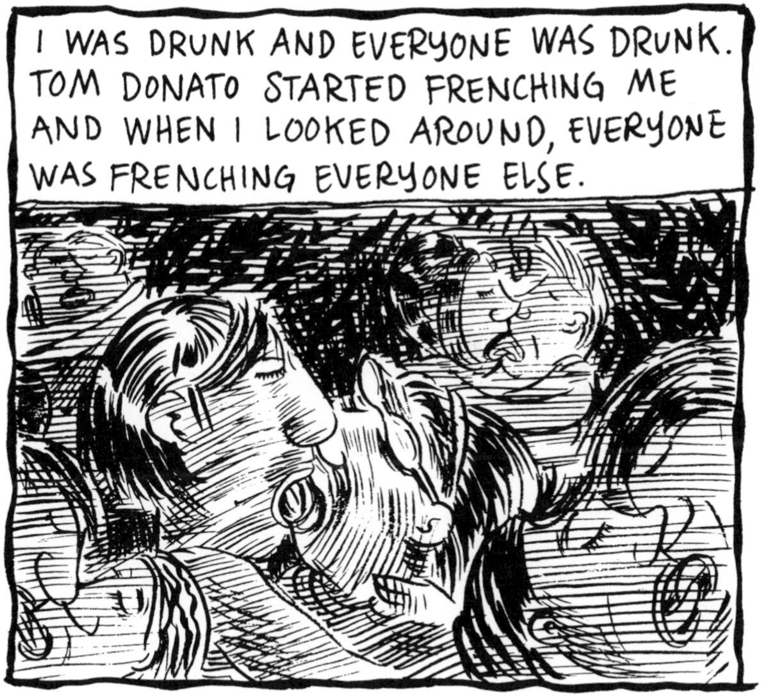
I WAS DRUNK AND EVERYONE WAS DRUNK. TOM DONATO STARTED FRENCHING ME AND WHEN I LOOKED AROUND, EVERYONE WAS FRENCHING EVERYONE ELSE.

"COME ON" TOM SAID. WE WENT BACK DEEPER IN THE WOODS. WE DRANK MORE JUNGLE JUICE AND WE WERE LAYING DOWN. STICKS AND BRANCHES WERE STICKING ME IN THE BACK.

HE KEPT TAKING MY HAND AND PUTTING IT IN HIS UNDERWEAR. I KEPT NOT DOING IT. HE KEPT SAYING "PLEASE, PLEASE" AND FINALLY I TOUCHED IT FOR ABOUT ONE MINUTE THEN HE SAT UP AND BARFED.

I ABOUT STARTED BARFING TOO. I COULD HARDLY WALK. I WENT OVER TO FIND MY COUSIN AND I STARTED CRYING FOR NO REASON AND TOLD ROYLTON TOM USED ME.

THEN I CAN'T HARDLY REMEMBER. SOME-ONE WAS FEELING ME UP AND I WAS CRYING. CINDY LUDERMYER WAS CRYING TOO BECAUSE SHE BARFED OUT HER RETAINER AND COULDN'T FIND IT.

AND THEN ALL OF A SUDDEN I WAS ON THE FOOT BRIDGE TRYING TO WALK HOME. IT WAS STARTING TO GET LIGHT. I WAS TALKING TO GOD OUT LOUD, TELLING HIM TO PLEASE JUST LET ME GET HOME.

IN THE A + W PARKING LOT I SAW MY DAD'S CAR. I TRIED CUTTING AROUND THE OTHER WAY BUT HE CAUGHT ME. "HI DAD." I SAID AND I THREW UP.

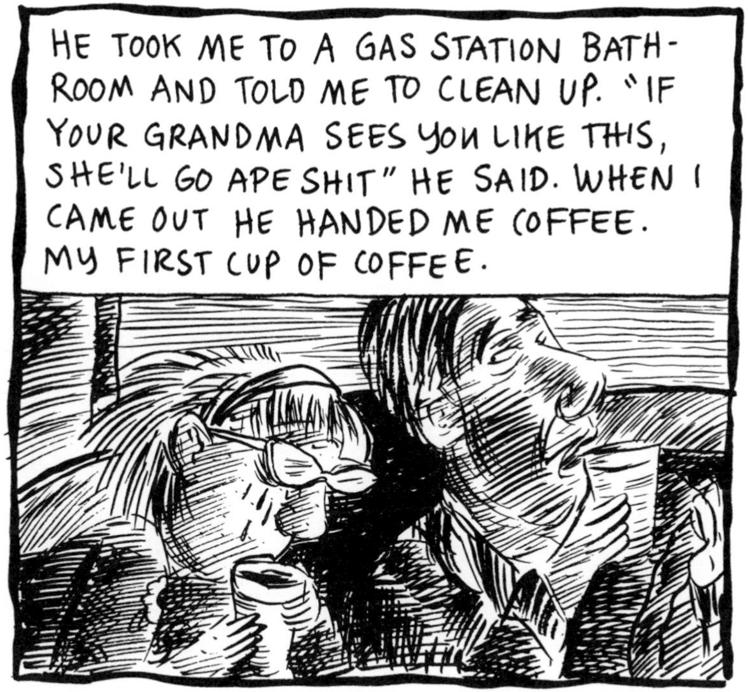
HE TOOK ME TO A GAS STATION BATH-ROOM AND TOLD ME TO CLEAN UP. "IF YOUR GRANDMA SEES YOU LIKE THIS, SHE'LL GO APE SHIT" HE SAID. WHEN I CAME OUT HE HANDED ME COFFEE. MY FIRST CUP OF COFFEE.

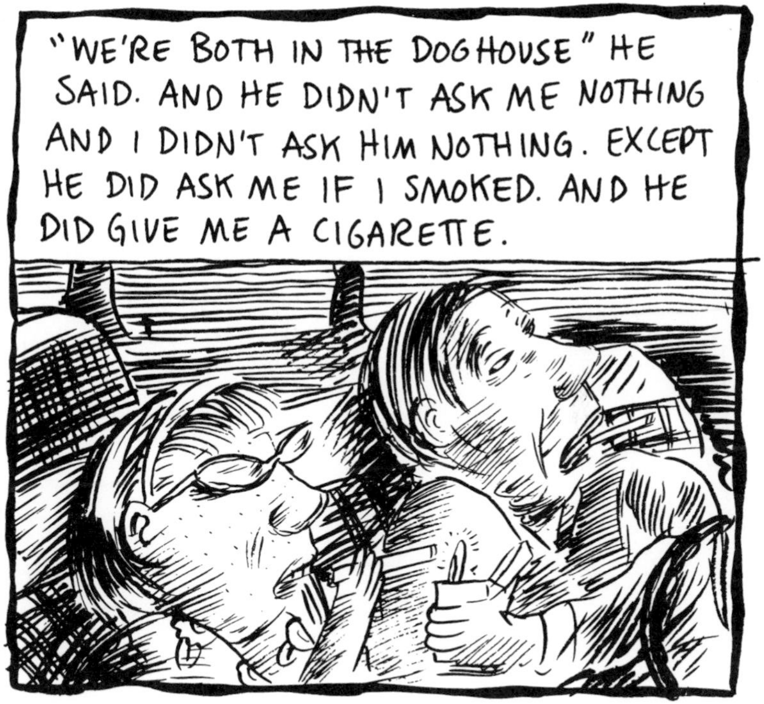
"WE'RE BOTH IN THE DOGHOUSE" HE SAID. AND HE DIDN'T ASK ME NOTHING AND I DIDN'T ASK HIM NOTHING. EXCEPT HE DID ASK ME IF I SMOKED. AND HE DID GIVE ME A CIGARETTE.

WE SAT IN THE CAR. HE TOLD ME WORK- ING FOR MR. LUDERMYER WAS KILLING HIM AND LIVING WITH GRANDMA WAS DRIVING HIM NUTS. I KNEW HE WAS LEAVING AGAIN. I KNEW IT.

IT WASN'T THE FIRST TIME HE LEFT AND IT WASN'T THE LAST TIME HE LEFT. HE SAID HE WAS GLAD I UNDERSTOOD. I COULDN'T SAY ANYTHING.

I'M LUCKY I GOT A KID LIKE YOU.

NO, LISTEN. I AM.

WHEN HE DROPPED ME OFF, HE TOLD ME THREE THINGS. TELL GRANDMA NOT TO WORRY, TELL MY SISTER HE LOVED HER, AND FOR ME TO CHEW ASPIRIN FOR MY HANGOVER.

BE GOOD. AND DON'T GIVE YOUR GRANDMA NO TROUBLE.

AND WHEN HIS CAR PULLED AWAY, I TURNED AROUND AND SAW MY GRANDMA AND MR. LUDERMYER STANDING IN THE PICTURE WINDOW.

109

THE WORLD OF MY LIFE

L · Y · N · D · A · B · A · R · R · Y · © · 1989 ·

DEAR BRENDA, HI. WHAT'S HAPPENING? MY MOM SENT YOUR LETTER HERE. IT WAS A BEAUTIFUL LETTER AND IT'S BEAUTIFUL THAT YOU WANT TO BE FRIENDS AGAIN. I FELT MESSED UP FOR A LONG TIME BY US NOT BEING FRIENDS BUT PLEASE DON'T FEEL GUILTY ABOUT EVERYTHING YOU DID.

I HARDLY EVEN THINK ABOUT HOW YOU MESSED UP MY LIFE LAST YEAR. I ONLY THINK ABOUT YOUR GOOD PART THAT I KNOW WAS STILL SECRETLY MY FRIEND THE WHOLE TIME YOU WERE BEING SO COLD TO ME WITH SANDY ALFANO THAT I ALMOST COMMITTED SUICIDE. SO DON'T EVEN FEEL GUILTY! IT'S A BEAUTIFUL DAY!

YOU PROBABLY HEARD THAT ME AND MARLYS HAD TO MOVE OUT TO MY GRANDMAS. IT REALLY SUCKS OUT HERE. MY GRANDMA DOESN'T SUCK, BUT EVERYTHING ELSE DOES. INCLUDING PEOPLE. IT'S TOTALLY WHITE AND PREJUDICED FOR ONE THING. THEY DON'T EVEN KNOW WHAT'S SOUL POWER!

MY SCHOOL IS SELMER JR. HIGH WHICH SUCKS ALSO. I INVENTED THIS THING ABOUT IT. "S TO THE 4TH POWER." IT STANDS FOR: "SELMER SUCKS SO SERIOUSLY." SO WHEN YOU SEE S^4, YOU WILL GET IT. I'LL WRITE MORE LATER BECAUSE I'M IN BORING MATH AND HE WANTS US TO PAY ATTENTION. MR. SEMIEN. I'M NOT KIDDING, THAT'S HIS NAME.
S^4 S^4 S^4 LOVE YA, Maybonne S^4 S^4 S^4

HOME EC

L·Y·N·D·A·B·A·R·R·Y· © 1989

DEAR BRENDA, HI! I HAVE A REALLY BORING CLASS RIGHT NOW, MISS RAYBURN HOME EC. YOU SHOULD SEE HER. SHE THINKS SHE IS SO MOD. BUT SHE ISN'T.

SHE IS REALLY SKINNY AND KEEPS TALKING ABOUT HOW SHE HAD TO PICK BETWEEN FASHION MODEL OR HOME EC TEACHER. IN HER DREAMS.!! AS IF YOU WOULD EVER PICK HOME EC TEACHER! SHE IS SO IN LOVE WITH HERSELF! RIGHT NOW WE ARE ON GOOD GROOMING. HANG ON SHE'S COMING OVER BY MY DESK.

WHITE LIPSTICK MAKES YOU LOOK LIKE A CORPSE.

IS THAT THE EFFECT YOU WISH TO CREATE?

IT'S LATER ON. WE'RE DOING MINI-REPORTS. I'M SUPPOSED TO BE WRITING A THING ON PERSPIRATION BUT THIS ONE GIRL AT MY TABLE KEEPS ON HOGGING THE BOOK! DID YOU KNOW THAT SWEAT DOESN'T SMELL, IT'S BACTERIA? KIND OF A FREAK OUT WHEN YOU THINK OF BACTERIA = B.O.

OH MAN. MISS RAYBURN IS JUST NOW HAVING A TOTAL COW BECAUSE SOMEONE STOLE HER ROCK WITH THE EYES PAINTED ON IT. IT WAS A ROCK WITH EYES PAINTED ON THAT SAID "SMILE" AND IT WAS ON HER DESK AND SOMEONE KYPED IT. I HAVE TO GO SHES LOOKING IN EVERYONES PURSE. LOVE YA! SELMER JR. HIGH SUCKS! Maybonne

RINGGG!

IGNORE THE BELL AND REMAIN SEATED!

WE WILL SIT HERE ALL NIGHT IF WE HAVE TO!

SORROW + HAPPINESS

BY LYNDA BARRY © 1989

IN HEALTH WE'RE DOING THE DIGESTIVE SYSTEM. WE EACH GOT ASSIGNED A TOPIC FOR AN ORAL REPORT. I GOT THE SMALL INTESTINE. I SWEAR TO GOD I HATE MY LIFE.

much of the pain and sorrow and so much of the pleasure and happiness of life are tied up with the condition of the digestive tract that it is highly that we keep it in the ing or

I TRIED TRADING WITH THE GIRL WHO GOT THE STOMACH BUT NO WAY. SAME WITH GASTRIC JUICE. THE ONLY ONE WHO WILL TRADE HAS THE LARGE IN-TESTINE. I AM NOT TAKING THE LARGE INTESTINE.

C'MON. YOU SAID YOU WANTED TO TRADE.

NO MAN. THAT'S OK.

MRS. SPENCE SAID TELL THE STORY LIKE YOU ARE THE FOOD USING CONTRASTS AND COMPARISONS. AS I ENTER THE SMALL INTESTINE I GET SQUEEZED BY MUSCLES. IT'S DARK AND THE WALLS LOOK LIKE SLIMEY CRUSHED VELVET. THERE'S PANCREAS JUICE ON ME, HELP ME, I AM DISINTEGRATING.

HOW LONG WILL THIS TORTURE GO ON? FOR 20 FEET IN AN ADULT MALE. ~ ON THE DAY OF THE REPORTS THE LARGE INTESTINE WAS ABSENT. ALSO THE GASTRIC JUICE. I DID MINE AND PEOPLE LIKED IT. I GOT AN A. I BELIEVE IN GOD THE FATHER ALMIGHTY CREATOR OF HEAVEN AND EARTH.

MANNERS

BY LYNDA · BARRY © 1989

HI BRENDA! WHAT IT IS. I'M IN HOME EC. WE GOT OUR BOOKS. YOU WOULD BARF FROM THE TITLE: "SO YOU ARE GOING TO BE A TEEN." AS IF! SHE GOES "LADIES, PLEASE TURN TO MANNERS. PAGE 101." RIGHT?

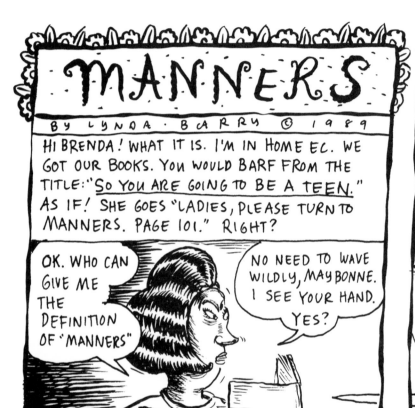

OK. WHO CAN GIVE ME THE DEFINITION OF "MANNERS"

NO NEED TO WAVE WILDLY, MAYBONNE. I SEE YOUR HAND. YES?

WHEN I OPEN MINE, THERES A BIG WAD OF FOOD SMASHED IN THE CRACK SO I SAY I WANT A NEW BOOK AND MISS RAYBURN GOES NO. THEN I ACCIDENTLY SLAM MY BOOK DOWN RIGHT? AND SHE HAS A COW. SHE PUTS MY NAME ON THE BOARD IN THIS LAME THING OF HERS CALLED "GRUMPIES AND GROUCHES" AND I HAVE TO DO LUNCH-ROOM CLEAN UP. LAME! LAME LAME LAME! LAME TO THE 10,000,000 POWER!

MISS RAYBURN THERE'S CHUNKS OF FOOD IN MY BOOK.

THAT'S NOT AN ANSWER TO MY QUESTION, MAYBONNE.

SO WE'RE SUPPOSED TO WRITE THE ABC'S OF TABLE MANNERS SO I FINISH EARLY THEN I START DOING A JOKE VERSION OF THEM. ANYONE COULD SEE IT WAS A JOKE !!!!

(A)lways chew with your mouth open!

(B)e sure to grab food from others!

tell the hostess the food looks (C)orroded!

tell the hostess she needs (D)eoderent!

tell your hostess her dentures need (E)fferdent!

(F)ood is for playing with!

(G)o "this sucks" to all the food!

tell your hostess she has (H)alitosis

SHE BUSTS ME FOR IT AND TELLS ME I'M DISRESPECTFUL OF THE CONCEPT OF HER CLASS! WHAT DOES THAT EVEN MEAN? SHE TRIES TO SINGE ME BY MAKING ME READ IT OUT LOUD BUT THE SINGE WAS ON HER BECAUSE PEOPLE STARTED CRACKING UP AT MY JOKES! THEN SHE SAID COPY THE WHOLE MANNERS CHAPTER! SHE THINKS I'M COPYING IT NOW! HA HA HA HA HA HA MISS RAYBURN! I HATE THIS SCHOOL! WRITE BACK! LOVE ya. Maybonne

WHAT?

I'M DOING IT!

TOPIC: HAIR

BY LYNDA BARRY. © 1989 CHICAGO, ILL.

HAIR

Maybonne
Home Ec. Period 3

Topic Hair

1. What is hair?
   Hair is a projection growing off of a mammel. A certain kind of projection. It has many uses. It grows on every Mammel.

THE HAIR

oil gland

Root   Shaft   Split end

follicle

2. What is the best hairstyle for you? It depends on your ~~face head~~ face head. Give some examples of hairstyles for
3. the different shapes of heads.

1. Long

DO
try to get fullness
Bangs are good. Curl for fullness.

YES

DON'T
Just let it hang straight. Your head will look worse.

NO

2. Round

YES

DO Let it hang down pretty straight to cover sides of head. Curl the ends.

DON'T Curl it on top of your head unless you want to be a bowling ball head !!

NO

3. _Pearshaped._

Do. BAlance by fullness at the top. Remember the goal is to look normal.

YES

Dont let your hair come down and help emphasize the weird shape.

NO

#5

4. _Upside down_ Pear face

Do. make it full at the bottom →

YES

Don't pile it up on top.

NO

Remember: Try to make your hair do the tricks the shape of your head doesn't know how to.

5. What is good for your hair?
Foods: milk, egg yolks, animal livers, oils
              eating

6. Fact or Myth^ jello will make your hair grow.
   Myth

7. What are good things to do to your hair?
brushing, shampoo, creme rinse, a sensible hairstyle that does not look rediculous

8. What are bad things to do to your hair?
ratting. Too much sun in. Ironing it.
wearing a fall that doesn't match.
letting your friend cut it.
~~think~~ you are cool because it looks good.
thinking

9. What have you learned from this chapter?
   I have a weird shaped head but I
   can correct it with hair. Also hair is dead.

119

STRING HEADS

· L · y · N · D · A · B · A · R · R · y · © 89

DEAR BRENDA, REMEMBER I TOLD YOU ABOUT MISS RAYBURN? I HATE HER. SHE PUT ME AND THIS GIRL NANCY NEWBY ON LUNCHROOM DUTY. I GOT IT BECAUSE I ACCIDENTLY SLAMMED MY BOOK DOWN. NANCY GOT IT BECAUSE SHE ACCIDENTLY SAID "HOME EC SUCKS" AND MISS RAYBURN WAS BY HER.

IF THEY GIVE YOU ANY TROUBLE...

CALL ME.

I SURELY WILL!

YOU HAVE TO WEAR A DORKED OUT APRON. ALSO, A HAIRNET. I SAID NO WAY AM I WEARING A HAIRNET. THEN THEY SAID OK GO TO THE VICE PRINCIPAL. NANCY NEWBY IS COOL SHE SAID SHE WASN'T WEARING A HAIRNET EITHER SO THEN WE BOTH GOT SENT UP TO MR. VALOTTOS WHO SAID DID WE WANT TO GET SUSPENDED.

(THINKS HE'S) HIP

(SIDEBURNS)

(TURTLE NECK DICKEY)

YOU GIRLS BETTER GET WITH WHAT'S GOING DOWN! I AM NOT A JIVE TURKEY AND THIS SCHOOL IS NOT A JIVE TURKEY! ANY QUESTIONS?

(COMMUNICATION)

SO WE PUT ON THE HAIRNETS THEN NANCY NEWBY STARTS GOING "WE ARE THE STRING HEADS WE ARE THE STRING **HEADS**" IN THIS VOICE OF A ROBOT AND I WAS PEEING MY PANTS FROM IT. WE WERE CARRYING TRAYS AND THEN I DROPPED MY TRAYS THEN SHE DROPPED HER TRAYS THEN NO WAY COULD WE STOP LAUGHING. YOU KNOW THAT THING WHEN YOU CAN'T STOP LAUGHING?

SO THEN WE GOT SENT TO MR. VALOTTOS WHO ASKED US DID WE THINK WE COULD CONTROL OUR BEHAVIOR, BECAUSE ONE MORE PINK SLIP AND <u>SUSPENSION</u>. AFTER SCHOOL NANCY NEWBY CAME OVER. SHE SMOKES NEWPORTS. SHE SHOWED ME HOW SHE STOLE THE HAIRNET, IT WAS IN HER PURSE. I THINK SHE'S GOING TO BE ALL RIGHT AS A FRIEND. PLEASE WRITE BACK SOON. S4S4S4 LUV YA, maybonne

SOME FEELINGS

LO YO NO NO A. ® OB O AO RO RO YO © 89

DEAR BRENDA, DID I EVER TELL YOU ABOUT MY COUSIN HERE THAT'S MARRIED, DONNA BUCSKO? SHE ALWAYS WANTS ME TO COME OVER BECAUSE SHE IS BORED WITH HER LIFE. SHE LIVES ON SOUTH DOYLE. HER STREET IS KIND OF SUCKY.

HEYA MAYBONNE

HEYA DONNA

HER HOUSE SUCKS TOO. MY GRANDMA SAYS SHE'S AN EXAMPLE. HER HUSBAND IS KEN. GOD THAT IS <u>WEIRD</u> TO WRITE "<u>HER HUSBAND</u>" BECAUSE DONNA'S ONLY <u>3 YEARS OLDER</u> <u>THAN</u> <u>US</u>! KEN IS OK, HIS ONLY PROBLEM IS <u>WHAT</u> <u>A</u> <u>SLOB</u>! HE THINKS DONNA'S HIS <u>PERSONAL</u> <u>MAID</u>! AND I KNOW THIS SOUNDS COLD BUT THEIR BABY IS UGLY. A <u>GIANT</u> FOREHEAD, I FEEL BAD SAYING IT.

OH HELL. HOLD HIM FOR A SECOND.

DING-DONG!

YEAH

OK.

DONNA SMOKES AND WANT TO KNOW A WEIRD THING? EVEN THOUGH SHES MARRIED SHE STILL CAN'T BUY CIGS! THE NEIGHBOR MARIE HAS TO BUY THEM FOR HER WHICH DONNA HATES BECAUSE MARIE TALKS DONNA'S HEAD OFF! IF YOU COULD SEE MARIES EYEBROWS! MARIES HUSBAND DIED. DONNA SAID FROM MARIE'S TALKING! MARIE ALSO HAS A GIANT FOREHEAD.

GOOD GOD I TELL YA IF STANLEY WERE LIVING TODAY HE WOULDN'T STAND FOR THE RIFF RAFF MOVIN' IN. OH LORD DON'T GET ME STARTED. HOLY BALLS! WHAT THE HELL IS THIS WORLD COMING TO

ME AND DONNA ALWAYS MAKE CHEF BOY ARDEE PIZZA. SHE PUTS SLICED HOT DOGS ON IT FOR THE MEAT. THE BABY IS NAMED GENE. SHE PUT A PIECE OF HOT DOG IN HIS MOUTH TO SEE IF HE WOULD EAT HOT DOGS YET AND HE STARTED CHOKING AND SHE HUNG HIM UPSIDE DOWN AND THE HOT DOG FELL ON THE RUG. DONNA SAYS THE ONE GOOD THING ABOUT HER LIFE IS NO MORE SCHOOL. LUV ya

maybonne

KNOWING things

· L Y N D A · B A R R Y · © 1989

MY SISTER MARLYS IS DOING A PROJECT OUT ON THE BACK PORCH ABOUT PLANTS. SHE'S ONLY 8 SO SHE'S STILL NOT SICK OF KNOWING THINGS. I DID THAT SAME PROJECT ABOUT A MILLION YEARS AGO. YOU PLANT BEANS IN A MILK CARTON. BIG DEAL.

I KEEP TELLIN' YOU. YOU'RE NOT DOIN' IT RIGHT.

BUG OFF.

I TOLD HER SHE ONLY NEEDS THREE TO DO THE EXPERIMENT OF ① NO WATER. ② SOME WATER. ③ FLOODING. SHE PLANTED 30. SHE'S TRYING KOOLAID, MILK, AND CRAGMONT ROOT BEER. SHE RUBBED ONE WITH VICKS. SHE PUT MILK DUDS IN THE DIRT OF ONE. SHE SAYS SHE'S LOOKING FOR THE SECRET FORMULA.

I'M ♪ MILTON ♫ YOUR BRAND ♫ NEW SON ♫

WHEN I TRY TO TELL HER THERE'S NO WAY, SHE GOES: "THAT'S WHAT THEY ALL SAY." I DON'T KNOW WHERE SHE EVEN GOT THAT! IT'S FROM THE BOOKS YOU KEEP READING WITH NO REALITY IN THEM. A MAGIC TREE STARTS TALKING OR A MAGIC DOG STARTS TALKING AND EVERYTHING IN THE WORLD CAN BE MAGIC. EVEN YOUR SPIT CAN BE MAGIC. AND NOW THAT'S WHAT SHE THINKS. THERE'S ONE PLANT SHE SPITS ON.

I TRIED TO EXPLAIN TO HER THE CONCEPT OF REALITY AND THAT REALITY IS BEAUTIFUL AND SHE SAID HER PLANTS WERE REALITY AND SHE WAS REALITY AND HER EXPERIMENTS WERE REALITY AND I SAID THE REAL REALITY WAS SHE WAS THE TORTURER OF PLANTS AND ALL THE PLANTS WERE GOING TO DIE BECAUSE OF HER AND WHAT I SAID CAME TRUE. IT CAME TRUE. IT CAME TRUE. MARLYS, I'M SORRY IT CAME TRUE.

125

the SURPRISE

LYNDA BARRY ✿✿✿✿✿ © 1990 ✿✿✿✿✿

DEAR BRENDA, SORRY I DIDN'T WRITE FOR SO LONG BUT MY LIFE WENT ON SUCH A DOWNER. IF YOU CAN RELATE TO THAT. BEING ON A DOWNER THAT KEEPS LASTING. THIS HAS BEEN SUCH A WEIRDED OUT YEAR. LIVING WITH MY GRANDMA IS O.K. BUT EVEN THOUGH I KNOW MOM HATES ME, I STILL WISH I WAS LIVING BACK WITH HER AND HANGING AROUND YOU.

ALSO I STARTED CONSIDERING THE WHOLE DOWNER OF THE WHOLE WORLD. ITS STILL THE SAME PROBLEMS. VIOLENCE, PREJUDICE AND POLLUTION. EXACTLY LIKE IN THE SONG "WHAT'S GOING ON." TRUTHFULLY ITS HARD SOMETIMES TO KEEP ON TRUCKIN', BUT LIKE THAT THING WHERE THEY SAY "KEEP THE FAITH BABY," I AM TRYING. ONE THING THOUGH I AM NOT SURE ABOUT NOW THOUGH, IS GOD.

HAVE YOU READ THAT THING ON ANNE FRANK IN YOUR CLASS YET? SHE WAS OUR SAME AGE ISN'T THAT WEIRD. I HAD TO WRITE A PAPER ON IT AND I PRAYED TO GOD FOR AN EXPLANATION OF THE THING, BUT BRENDA HE DIDN'T SAY NOTHING TO ME BACK. I KNOW I AM PROBABLY LIKE AN ANT TO HIM AND BIG DEAL ABOUT MY PAPER BUT LOOK WHAT HE SAID TO ANNE FRANK WHEN SHE PRAYED AND MILLIONS OF OTHER PEOPLE AND NOT JUST THEM BUT HOW ABOUT BACK DURING THE SLAVES? BECAUSE I KNOW THEY PRAYED TOO.

IF YOU CAN BELIEVE IT, ITS 3AM WHEN I'M WRITING THIS. MY SISTER MARLYS IS IN THE BED SLEEPING AND THE WEIRDEST THING JUST HAPPENED. OUTSIDE MY WINDOW I HEARD A BIRD SINGING IN THE PITCH BLACK. IF RIGHT NOW WAS A MOVIE WHERE A GIRL WAS WRITING YOU THIS LETTER ABOUT THESE QUESTIONS, I GUESS THAT WOULD MEAN SOMETHING. I DON'T KNOW. MAYBE THE SURPRISE ABOUT GOD IS THAT HE IS SMALL. MAYBE ALL HE CAN SAY IS KEEP YOUR EYES PEELED FOR PROBLEMS AND HELP EACH OTHER AND BE CAREFUL WHERE YOU GET YOUR INSTRUCTIONS. WELL THAT'S ALL I KNOW TO WRITE. I HOPE YOU ARE DOING GOOD.

PEACE + LOVE,
Maybonne

P.S. I still think life is magical.

Lynda Barry has worked as a painter, cartoonist, writer, illustrator, playwright, editor, commentator, and teacher and finds that they are all very much alike. She lives in Wisconsin, where she is Professor of Interdisciplinary Creativity at the University of Wisconsin-Madison.

Barry is the author of *The Freddie Stories*, *One! Hundred! Demons!*, *The! Greatest! of! Marlys!*, *Cruddy: An Illustrated Novel*, and *The Good Times are Killing Me*, which was adapted as an off-Broadway play and won the Washington State Governor's Award.

She has written four bestselling and acclaimed creative how-to graphic novels for Drawn & Quarterly: *What It Is*, which won an Eisner Award and the RR Donnelley Literary Award for highest literary achievement by a Wisconsin author; *Picture This*; *Syllabus: Notes From an Accidental Professor*; and the two Eisner Award-winning *Making Comics*. In 2019, she was named a MacArthur Fellow.

The stories in *Come Over Come Over* were originally serialized as *Ernie Pook's Comeek* in the *Chicago Reader* and other alternative weeklies across the USA between 1988–1990. "Sneaking Out" was originally published in *Raw* magazine in 1990.